THE

# DIVINE TRAGEDY

BY

HENRY WADSWORTH LONGFELLOW

BOSTON
JAMES R. OSGOOD AND COMPANY
1871

UNIVERSITY PRESS: WELCH, BIGELOW, & CO.,
CAMBRIDGE.

# CONTENTS.

## THE THIRD PASSOVER.

# INTROITUS

*The* ANGEL *bearing the* PROPHET HABAKKUK *through
the air.*

PROPHET.

WHY dost thou bear me aloft,
    O Angel of God, on thy pinions
O'er realms and dominions?
Softly I float as a cloud
In air, for thy right hand upholds me,
Thy garment enfolds me!

ANGEL.

Lo! as I passed on my way
In the harvest-field I beheld thee,
When no man compelled thee,
Bearing with thine own hands
This food to the famishing reapers,
A flock without keepers!

The fragrant sheaves of the wheat
Made the air above them sweet;
Sweeter and more divine
Was the scent of the scattered grain,

I

That the reaper's hand let fall
To be gathered again
By the hand of the gleaner!
Sweetest, divinest of all,
Was the humble deed of thine,
And the meekness of thy demeanor!

PROPHET.

Angel of Light,
I cannot gainsay thee,
I can but obey thee!

ANGEL.

Beautiful was it in the Lord's sight,
To behold his Prophet
Feeding those that toil,
The tillers of the soil.
But why should the reapers eat of it
And not the Prophet of Zion
In the den of the lion?
The Prophet should feed the Prophet!
Therefore I thee have uplifted,
And bear thee aloft by the hair
Of thy head, like a cloud that is drifted
Through the vast unknown of the air!

Five days hath the Prophet been lying
In Babylon, in the den
Of the lions, death-defying,

Defying hunger and thirst ;
But the worst
Is the mockery of men !
Alas ! how full of fear
Is the fate of Prophet and Seer !
Forevermore, forevermore,
It shall be as it hath been heretofore ;
The age in which they live
Will not forgive
The splendor of the everlasting light, .
That makes their foreheads bright,
Nor the sublime
Fore-running of their time !

PROPHET.

O tell me, for thou knowest,
Wherefore and by what grace,
Have I, who am least and lowest,
Been chosen to this place,
To this exalted part ?

ANGEL.

Because thou art
The Struggler ; and from thy youth
Thy humble and patient life
Hath been a strife
And battle for the Truth ;
Nor hast thou paused nor halted,
Nor ever in thy pride

Turned from the poor aside,
But with deed and word and pen
Hast served thy fellow-men ;
Therefore art thou exalted !

PROPHET.

By thine arrow's light
Thou goest onward through the night,
And by the clear
Sheen of thy glittering spear !
When will our journey end ?

ANGEL.

Lo, it is ended !
Yon silver gleam
Is the Euphrates stream.
Let us descend
Into the city splendid,
Into the City of Gold !

PROPHET.

Behold !
As if the stars had fallen from their places
Into the firmament below,
The streets, the gardens, and the vacant spaces
With light are all aglow ;
And hark !
As we draw near,
What sound is it I hear
Ascending through the dark ?

### ANGEL.

The tumultuous noise of the nations,
Their rejoicings and lamentations,
The pleadings of their prayer,
The groans of their despair,
The cry of their imprecations,
Their wrath, their love, their hate !

### PROPHET.

Surely the world doth wait
The coming of its Redeemer !

### ANGEL.

Awake from thy sleep, O dreamer !
The hour is near, though late ;
Awake ! write the vision sublime,
The vision, that is for a time,
Though it tarry, wait; it is nigh ;
In the end it will speak and not lie.

# THE DIVINE TRAGEDY

## THE FIRST PASSOVER

# THE DIVINE TRAGEDY

---

## I.

### VOX CLAMANTIS.

#### JOHN THE BAPTIST.

REPENT! repent! repent!
For the kingdom of God is at hand,
And all the land
Full of the knowledge of the Lord shall be
As the waters cover the sea,
And encircle the continent!

Repent! repent! repent!
For lo, the hour appointed,
The hour so long foretold
By the Prophets of old,
Of the coming of the Anointed,
The Messiah, the Paraclete,
The Desire of the Nations, is nigh!
He shall not strive nor cry,
Nor his voice be heard in the street;
Nor the bruised reed shall he break,
Nor quench the smoking flax;
And many of them that sleep

In the dust of earth shall awake,
On that great and terrible day,
And the wicked shall wail and weep,
And be blown like a smoke away,
And be melted away like wax.
Repent! repent! repent!

O Priest, and Pharisee,
Who hath warned you to flee
From the wrath that is to be?
From the coming anguish and ire?
The axe is laid at the root
Of the trees, and every tree
That bringeth not forth good fruit
Is hewn down and cast into the fire!

Ye Scribes, why come ye hither?
In the hour that is uncertain,
In the day of anguish and trouble,
He that stretcheth the heavens as a curtain
And spreadeth them out as a tent,
Shall blow upon you, and ye shall wither,
And the whirlwind shall take you away as stubble!
Repent! repent! repent!

PRIEST.

Who art thou, O man of prayer!
In raiment of camel's hair,
Begirt with leathern thong,

That here in the wilderness,
With a cry as of one in distress,
Preachest unto this throng?
Art thou the Christ?

JOHN.

Priest of Jerusalem,
In meekness and humbleness,
I deny not, I confess
I am not the Christ!

PRIEST.

What shall we say unto them
That sent us here?    Reveal
Thy name, and naught conceal!
Art thou Elias?

JOHN.
No!
PRIEST.

Art thou that Prophet, then,
Of lamentation and woe,
Who, as a symbol and sign
Of impending wrath divine
Upon unbelieving men,
Shattered the vessel of clay
In the Valley of Slaughter?

JOHN.
Nay.

I am not he thou namest!

PRIEST.

Who art thou, and what is the word
That here thou proclaimest?

JOHN.

I am the voice of one
Crying in the wilderness alone :
Prepare ye the way of the Lord ;
Make his paths straight
In the land that is desolate !

PRIEST.

If thou be not the Christ,
Nor yet Elias, nor he
That, in sign of the things to be,
Shattered the vessel of clay
In the Valley of Slaughter,
Then declare unto us, and say
By what authority now
Baptizest thou?

JOHN.

I indeed baptize you with water
Unto repentance ; but He,
That cometh after me,
Is mightier than I and higher ;
The latchet of whose shoes
I am not worthy to unloose ;
He shall baptize you with fire,
And with the Holy Ghost !

Whose fan is in his hand ;
He will purge to the uttermost
His floor, and garner his wheat,
But will burn the chaff in the brand
And fire of unquenchable heat !
Repent ! repent ! repent !


## II.

### MOUNT QUARANTANIA.

#### I.

##### LUCIFER.

NOT in the lightning's flash, nor in the thunder,
Not in the tempest, nor the cloudy storm,
    Will I array my form ;
But part invisible these boughs asunder,
And move and murmur, as the wind upheaves
    And whispers in the leaves.

Not as a terror and a desolation,
Not in my natural shape, inspiring fear
    And dread, will I appear ;
But in soft tones of sweetness and persuasion,
A sound as of the fall of mountain streams,
    Or voices heard in dreams.

He sitteth there in silence, worn and wasted
With famine, and uplifts his hollow eyes
    To the unpitying skies ;

For forty days and nights he hath not tasted
Of food or drink, his parted lips are pale,
    Surely his strength must fail.

Wherefore dost thou in penitential fasting
Waste and consume the beauty of thy youth?
    Ah, if thou be in truth
The Son of the Unnamed, the Everlasting,
Command these stones beneath thy feet to be
    Changed into bread for thee!


### CHRISTUS.

'T is written: Man shall not live by bread alone,
But by each word that from God's mouth pro-
        ceedeth!


### II.


### LUCIFER.

Too weak, alas! too weak is the temptation
For one whose soul to nobler things aspires
    Than sensual desires!
Ah, could I, by some sudden aberration,
Lead and delude to suicidal death
    This Christ of Nazareth!

Unto the holy Temple on Moriah,
With its resplendent domes, and manifold
    Bright pinnacles of gold,

Where they await thy coming, O Messiah!
Lo, I have brought thee! Let thy glory here
    Be manifest and clear.

Reveal thyself by royal act and gesture,
Descending with the bright triumphant host
    Of all the highermost
Archangels, and about thee as a vesture
The shining clouds, and all thy splendors show
    Unto the world below!

Cast thyself down, it is the hour appointed;
And God hath given his angels charge and care
    To keep thee and upbear
Upon their hands his only Son, the Anointed,
Lest he should dash his foot against a stone
    And die, and be unknown.

CHRISTUS.

'T is written: Thou shalt not tempt the Lord thy
    God!

III.

LUCIFER.

I cannot thus delude him to perdition!
But one temptation still remains untried,
    The trial of his pride,

The thirst of power, the fever of ambition !
Surely by these a humble peasant's son
    At last may be undone !

Above the yawning chasms and deep abysses,
Across the headlong torrents, I have brought
    Thy footsteps, swift as thought ;
And from the highest of these precipices,
The Kingdoms of the world thine eyes behold,
    Like a great map unrolled.

From far-off Lebanon, with cedars crested,
To where the waters of the Asphalt Lake
    On its white pebbles break,
And the vast desert, silent, sand-invested,
These kingdoms all are mine, and thine shall be,
    If thou wilt worship me !

CHRISTUS.

Get thee behind me, Satan ! thou shalt worship
The Lord thy God ; Him only shalt thou serve !

ANGELS MINISTRANT.

The sun goes down ; the evening shadows lengthen,
The fever and the struggle of the day
    Abate and pass away ;
Thine Angels Ministrant, we come to strengthen
And comfort thee, and crown thee with the palm,
    The silence and the calm.

## III.

### THE MARRIAGE IN CANA.

#### THE MUSICIANS.

Rise up, my love, my fair one,
Rise up, and come away,
For lo ! the winter is past,
The rain is over and gone,
The flowers appear on the earth,
The time of the singing of birds is come,
And the voice of the turtle is heard in our land.

#### THE BRIDEGROOM.

Sweetly the minstrels sing the Song of Songs !
My heart runs forward with it, and I say :
O set me as a seal upon thine heart,
And set me as a seal upon thine arm ;
For love is strong as life, and strong as death,
And cruel as the grave is jealousy !

#### THE MUSICIANS.

I sleep, but my heart awaketh ;
'T is the voice of my beloved
Who knocketh, saying : Open to me,
My sister, my love, my dove,
For my head is filled with dew,
My locks with the drops of the night !

#### THE BRIDE.

Ah yes, I sleep, and yet my heart awaketh,
It is the voice of my beloved who knocks.

2

### THE BRIDEGROOM.

O beautiful as Rebecca at the fountain,
O beautiful as Ruth among the sheaves !
O fairest among women ! O undefiled !
Thou art all fair, my love, there 's no spot in thee !

### THE MUSICIANS.

My beloved is white and ruddy,
The chiefest among ten thousand ;
His locks are black as a raven,
His eyes are the eyes of doves,
Of doves by the rivers of water,
His lips are like unto lilies,
Dropping sweet-smelling myrrh.

### ARCHITRICLINUS.

Who is that youth, with the dark azure eyes,
And hair, in color like unto the wine,
Parted upon his forehead, and behind
Falling in flowing locks?

### PARANYMPHUS.

The Nazarene
Who preacheth to the poor in field and village
The coming of God's Kingdom.

### ARCHITRICLINUS.

How serene
His aspect is ! manly yet womanly.

PARANYMPHUS.

Most beautiful among the sons of men!
Oft known to weep, but never known to laugh.

ARCHITRICLINUS.

And tell me, she with eyes of olive tint,
And skin as fair as wheat, and pale brown hair,
The woman at his side?

PARANYMPHUS.

             His mother, Mary.

ARCHITRICLINUS.

And the tall figure standing close behind them,
Clad all in white, with face and beard like ashes,
As if he were Elias, the White Witness,
Come from his cave on Carmel to foretell
The end of all things?

PARANYMPHUS.

             That is Manahem
The Essenian, he who dwells among the palms
Near the Dead Sea.

ARCHITRICLINUS.

             He who foretold to Herod
He should one day be King?

PARANYMPHUS.

             The same.

ARCHITRICLINUS.

Then why
Doth he come here to sadden with his presence
Our marriage feast, belonging to a sect
Haters of women, and that taste not wine?

THE MUSICIANS.

My undefiled is but one,
The only one of her mother,
The choice of her that bare her;
The daughters saw her and blessed her;
The queens and the concubines praised her,
Saying: Lo! who is this
That looketh forth as the morning?

MANAHEM, *aside.*

The Ruler of the Feast is gazing at me,
As if he asked, why is that old man here
Among the revellers?   And thou, the Anointed!
Why art thou here?   I see as in a vision
A figure clothed in purple, crowned with thorns;
I see a cross uplifted in the darkness,
And hear a cry of agony, that shall echo
Forever and forever through the world!

ARCHITRICLINUS.

Give us more wine.   These goblets are all empty.

MARY *to* CHRISTUS.

They have no wine!

CHRISTUS.

O woman, what have I
To do with thee?   Mine hour is not yet come.

MARY *to the servants*.

Whatever he shall say to you, that do.

CHRISTUS.

Fill up these pots with water.

THE MUSICIANS.

Come, my beloved,
Let us go forth into the field,
Let us lodge in the villages ;
Let us get up early to the vineyards,
Let us see if the vine flourish,
Whether the tender grape appear,
And the pomegranates bud forth.

CHRISTUS.

Draw out now
And bear unto the Ruler of the Feast.

MANAHEM, *aside*.

O thou, brought up among the Essenians,
Nurtured in abstinence, taste not the wine !
It is the poison of dragons from the vineyards
Of Sodom, and the taste of death is in it !

ARCHITRICLINUS *to the* BRIDEGROOM.

All men set forth good wine at the beginning ;

And when men have well drunk, that which is worse,
But thou hast kept the good wine until now.

MANAHEM, *aside.*

The things that have been and shall be no more,
The things that are, and that hereafter shall be,
The things that might have been, and yet were not,
The fading twilight of great joys departed,
The daybreak of great truths as yet unrisen,
The intuition and the expectation
Of something, which, when come, is not the same,
But only like its forecast in men's dreams,
The longing, the delay, and the delight,
Sweeter for the delay; youth, hope, love, death,
And disappointment which is also death,
All these make up the sum of human life;
A dream within a dream, a wind at night
Howling across the desert in despair,
Seeking for something lost, it cannot find.
Fate or foreseeing, or whatever name
Men call it, matters not; what is to be
Hath been fore-written in the thought divine
From the beginning.   None can hide from it,
But it will find him out; nor run from it,
But it o'ertaketh him!   The Lord hath said it.

THE BRIDEGROOM *to the* BRIDE, *on the balcony.*

When Abraham went with Sarah into Egypt,
The land was all illumined with her beauty;

But thou dost make the very night itself
Brighter than day!   Behold, in glad procession,
Crowding the threshold of the sky above us,
The stars come forth to meet thee with their lamps ;
And the soft winds, the ambassadors of flowers,
From neighboring gardens and from fields unseen,
Come laden with odors unto thee, my Queen !

### THE MUSICIANS.

Awake, O north-wind,
And come, thou wind of the South,
Blow, blow upon my garden,
That the spices thereof may flow out.

## IV.

### IN THE CORNFIELDS.

#### PHILIP.

ONWARD through leagues of sun-illumined corn,
As if through parted seas, the pathway runs,
And crowned with sunshine as the Prince of Peace
Walks the beloved Master, leading us,
As Moses led our fathers in old times
Out of the land of bondage !   We have found
Him of whom Moses and the Prophets wrote,
Jesus of Nazareth, the Son of Joseph.

NATHANAEL.

Can any good come out of Nazareth ?
Can this be the Messiah ?

PHILIP.

                        Come and see.

NATHANAEL.

The summer sun grows hot ; I am anhungered.
How cheerily the Sabbath-breaking quail
Pipes in the corn, and bids us to his Feast
Of Wheat Sheaves !   How the bearded, ripening ears
Toss in the roofless temple of the air ;
As if the unseen hand of some High-Priest
Waved them before Mount Tabor as an altar !
It were no harm, if we should pluck and eat.

PHILIP.

How wonderful it is to walk abroad
With the Good Master !   Since the miracle
He wrought at Cana, at the marriage feast,
His fame hath gone abroad through all the land,
And when we come to Nazareth, thou shalt see
How his own people will receive their Prophet,
And hail him as Messiah !   See, he turns
And looks at thee.

CHRISTUS.

                Behold an Israelite
In whom there is no guile.

NATHANAEL.

Whence knowest thou me?

CHRISTUS.

Before that Philip called thee, when thou wast
Under the fig-tree, I beheld thee.

NATHANAEL.

Rabbi!
Thou art the Son of God, thou art the King
Of Israel?

CHRISTUS.

Because I said I saw thee
Under the fig-tree, before Philip called thee,
Believest thou? Thou shalt see greater things.
Hereafter thou shalt see the heavens unclosed
And angels of God ascending and descending
Upon the Son of Man!

PHARISEES, *passing*.

Hail, Rabbi!

CHRISTUS.

Hail!

PHARISEES.

Behold how thy disciples do a thing
Which is not lawful on the Sabbath-day,
And thou forbiddest them not!

CHRISTUS.

Have ye not read
What David did when he anhungered was,
And all they that were with him? How he entered
Into the house of God, and ate the shewbread,
Which was not lawful saving for the priests?
Have ye not read, how on the Sabbath-days
The priests profane the Sabbath in the Temple,
And yet are blameless? But I say to you,
One in this place is greater than the Temple!
And had ye known the meaning of the words,
I will have mercy and not sacrifice,
The guiltless ye would not condemn. The Sabbath
Was made for man, and not man for the Sabbath.

*Passes on with the disciples.*

PHARISEES.

This is, alas! some poor demoniac
Wandering about the fields, and uttering
His unintelligible blasphemies
Among the common people, who receive
As prophecies the words they comprehend not!
Deluded folk! The incomprehensible
Alone excites their wonder. There is none
So visionary, or so void of sense,
But he will find a crowd to follow him!

## V.

### NAZARETH.

##### CHRISTUS, *reading in the Synagogue.*

THE Spirit of the Lord God is upon me.
He hath anointed me to preach good tidings
Unto the poor ; to heal the broken-hearted ;
To comfort those that mourn, and to throw open
The prison doors of captives, and proclaim
The Year Acceptable of the Lord, our God !

*He closes the book and sits down.*

##### A PHARISEE.

Who is this youth ?   He hath taken the Teacher's
    seat !
Will he instruct the Elders ?

##### A PRIEST.

Fifty years
Have I been Priest here in the Synagogue,
And never have I seen so young a man
Sit in the Teacher's seat !

##### CHRISTUS.

Behold, to-day
This scripture is fulfilled.   One is appointed
And hath been sent to them that mourn in Zion,
To give them beauty for ashes, and the oil
Of joy for mourning !   They shall build again

The old waste-places ; and again raise up
The former desolations, and repair
The cities that are wasted !   As a bridegroom
Decketh himself with ornaments ; as a bride
Adorneth herself with jewels, so the Lord
Hath clothed me with the robe of righteousness !

### A PRIEST.

He speaks the Prophet's words ; but with an air
As if himself had been foreshadowed in them !

### CHRISTUS.

For Zion's sake I will not hold my peace,
And for Jerusalem's sake I will not rest
Until its righteousness be as a brightness,
And its salvation as a lamp that burneth !
Thou shalt be called no longer the Forsaken,
Nor any more thy land, the Desolate.
The Lord hath sworn, by his right hand hath sworn,
And by his arm of strength : I will no more
Give to thine enemies thy corn as meat ;
The sons of strangers shall not drink thy wine.
Go through, go through the gates !   Prepare a way
Unto the people !   Gather out the stones !
Lift up a standard for the people !

### A PRIEST.

                                        Ah !

These are seditious words !

CHRISTUS.

And they shall call them
The holy people ; the redeemed of God !
And thou, Jerusalem, shalt be called Sought out,
A city not forsaken !


A PHARISEE.

Is not this
The carpenter Joseph's son ?   Is not his mother
Called Mary ? and his brethren and his sisters
Are they not with us ?   Doth he make himself
To be a Prophet ?


CHRISTUS.

No man is a Prophet
In his own country, and among his kin.
In his own house no Prophet is accepted.
I say to you, in the land of Israel
Were many widows in Elijah's day,
When for three years and more the heavens were
        shut,
And a great famine was throughout the land ;
But unto no one was Elijah sent
Save to Sarepta, to a city of Sidon,
And to a woman there that was a widow.
And many lepers were there in the land
Of Israel, in the time of Eliseus
The Prophet, and yet none of them was cleansed,
Save Naaman the Syrian !

A PRIEST.

Say no more!
Thou comest here into our Synagogue
And speakest to the Elders and the Priests,
As if the very mantle of Elijah
Had fallen upon thee!   Art thou not ashamed?

A PHARISEE.

We want no Prophets here!   Let him be driven
From Synagogue and city!   Let him go
And prophecy to the Samaritans!

AN ELDER.

The world is changed.   We Elders are as nothing!
We are but yesterdays, that have no part
Or portion in to-day!   Dry leaves that rustle,
That make a little sound, and then are dust!

A PHARISEE.

A carpenter's apprentice! a mechanic,
Whom we have seen at work here in the town
Day after day; a stripling without learning,
Shall he pretend to unfold the Word of God
To men grown old in study of the Law?

CHRISTUS *is thrust out.*

## VI.

### THE SEA OF GALILEE.

PETER *and* ANDREW *mending their nets.*

#### PETER.

NEVER was such a marvellous draught of fishes
Heard of in Galilee !   The market-places
Both of Bethsaida and Capernaum
Are full of them !   Yet we had toiled all night
And taken nothing, when the Master said :
Launch out into the deep, and cast your nets ;
And doing this, we caught such multitudes
Our nets like spiders' webs were snapped asunder,
And with the draught we filled two ships so full
That they began to sink.   Then I knelt down
Amazed, and said : O Lord, depart from me,
I am a sinful man.   And he made answer :
Simon, fear not ; henceforth thou shalt catch men !
What was the meaning of those words ?

#### ANDREW.

                     I know not.

But here is Philip, come from Nazareth.
He hath been with the Master.   Tell us, Philip,
What tidings dost thou bring ?

#### PHILIP.

                Most wonderful !

As we drew near to Nain, out of the gate

Upon a bier was carried the dead body
Of a young man, his mother's only son,
And she a widow, who with lamentation
Bewailed her loss, and the much people with her ;
And when the Master saw her he was filled
With pity ; and he said to her : Weep not !
And came and touched the bier, and they that
          bare it
Stood still ; and then he said : Young man, arise !
And he that had been dead sat up, and soon
Began to speak ; and he delivered him
Unto his mother.   And there came a fear
On all the people, and they glorified
The Lord, and said, rejoicing : A great Prophet
Is risen up among us ! and the Lord
Hath visited his people !


PETER.

                    A great Prophet ?
Ay, greater than a Prophet : greater even
Than John the Baptist !


PHILIP.

                    Yet the Nazarenes
Rejected him.


PETER.         •

          The Nazarenes are dogs !
As natural brute beasts, they growl at things
They do not understand ; and they shall perish,

Utterly perish in their own corruption.
The Nazarenes are dogs !

PHILIP.

They drave him forth
Out of their Synagogue, out of their city,
And would have cast him down a precipice,
But, passing through the midst of them, he van-
  ished
Out of their hands.

PETER.

Wells are they without water,
Clouds carried with a tempest, unto whom
The mist of darkness is reserved forever !

PHILIP.

Behold he cometh. There is one man with him
I am amazed to see !

ANDREW.

What man is that ?

PHILIP.

Judas Iscariot ; he that cometh last,
Girt with a leathern apron. No one knoweth
His history ; but the rumor of him is
He had an unclean spirit in his youth.
It hath not left him yet.

3

CHRISTUS, *passing*.

Come unto me,
All ye that labor and are heavy laden,
And I will give you rest !   Come unto me,
And take my yoke upon you and learn of me,
For I am meek, and I am lowly in heart,
And ye shall all find rest unto your souls !

PHILIP.

O, there is something in that voice that reaches
The innermost recesses of my spirit !
I feel that it might say unto the blind :
Receive your sight ! and straightway they would
    see !
I feel that it might say unto the dead,
Arise ! and they would hear it and obey !
Behold he beckons to us !

CHRISTUS, *to* PETER *and* ANDREW.

Follow me !

PETER.

Master, I will leave all and follow thee.

## VII.

### THE DEMONIAC OF GADARA.

A GADARENE.

HE hath escaped, hath plucked his chains asunder,
And broken his fetters ; always night and day
Is in the mountains here, and in the tombs,
Crying aloud, and cutting himself with stones,
Exceeding fierce, so that no man can tame him !

THE DEMONIAC *from above, unseen.*

O Aschmedai ! O Aschmedai, have pity !

A GADARENE.

Listen !   It is his voice !   Go warn the people
Just landing from the lake !

THE DEMONIAC.

O Aschmedai !
Thou angel of the bottomless pit, have pity !
It was enough to hurl King Solomon,
On whom be peace ! two hundred leagues away
Into the country, and to make him scullion,
In the kitchen of the King of Maschkemen !
Why dost thou hurl me here among these rocks,
And cut me with these stones ?

A GADARENE.

He raves and mutters
He knows not what.

THE DEMONIAC, *appearing from a tomb among the rocks.*

                  The wild cock Tarnegal
Singeth to me, and bids me to the banquet,
Where all the Jews shall come ; for they have slain
Behemoth the great ox, who daily cropped
A thousand hills for food, and at a draught
Drank up the river Jordan, and have slain
The huge Leviathan, and stretched his skin
Upon the high walls of Jerusalem,
And made them shine from one end of the world
Unto the other ; and the fowl Barjuchne,
Whose outspread wings eclipse the sun, and make
Midnight at noon o'er all the continents !
And we shall drink the wine of Paradise
From Adam's cellars.

A GADARENE.

             O, thou unclean spirit !

THE DEMONIAC, *hurling down a stone.*

This is the wonderful Barjuchne's egg,
That fell out of her nest, and broke to pieces,
And swept away three hundred cedar-trees,
And threescore villages !— Rabbi Eliezer,
How thou didst sin there in that seaport town,
When thou hadst carried safe thy chest of silver
Over the seven rivers for her sake !
I too have sinned beyond the reach of pardon.
Ye hills and mountains, pray for mercy on me !

Ye stars and planets, pray for mercy on me !
Ye sun and moon, O pray for mercy on me !

CHRISTUS *and his disciples pass.*

### A GADARENE.

There is a man here of Decapolis,
Who hath an unclean spirit ; so that none
Can pass this way.   He lives among the tombs
Up there upon the cliffs, and hurls down stones
On those who pass beneath.

### CHRISTUS.

Come out of him,
Thou unclean spirit !

### THE DEMONIAC.

What have I to do
With thee, thou Son of God ?   Do not torment us.

### CHRISTUS.

What is thy name ?

### DEMONIAC.

Legion ; for we are many.
Cain, the first murderer ; and the King Belshazzar,
And Evil Merodach of Babylon,
And Admatha, the death-cloud, prince of Persia ;
And Aschmedai, the angel of the pit,
And many other devils.   We are Legion.

Send us not forth beyond Decapolis ;
Command us not to go into the deep !
There is a herd of swine here in the pastures,
Let us go into them.

CHRISTUS.

Come out of him,
Thou unclean spirit !

A GADARENE.

See, how stupefied,
How motionless he stands !   He cries no more ;
He seems bewildered and in silence stares
As one who, walking in his sleep, awakes
And knows not where he is, and looks about him,
And at his nakedness, and is ashamed.

THE DEMONIAC.

Why am I here alone among the tombs ?
What have they done to me, that I am naked ?
Ah, woe is me !

CHRISTUS.

Go home unto thy friends
And tell them how great things the Lord hath done
For thee, and how he had compassion on thee !

A SWINEHERD, *running.*

The herds ! the herds ! O most unlucky day !
They were all feeding quiet in the sun,

When suddenly they started, and grew savage
As the wild boars of Tabor, and together
Rushed down a precipice into the sea!
They are all drowned!

PETER.

                Thus righteously are punished
The apostate Jews, that eat the flesh of swine,
And broth of such abominable things!

GREEKS OF GADARA.

We sacrifice a sow unto Demeter
At the beginning of harvest, and another
To Dionysus at the vintage-time.
Therefore we prize our herds of swine, and count
      them
Not as unclean, but as things consecrate
To the immortal gods.　O great magician,
Depart out of our coasts ; let us alone,
We are afraid of thee !

PETER.

               Let us depart ;
For they that sanctify and purify
Themselves in gardens, eating flesh of swine,
And the abomination, and the mouse,
Shall be consumed together, saith the Lord !

## VIII.

### TALITHA CUMI.

JAIRUS *at the feet of* CHRISTUS.

O MASTER ! I entreat thee ! I implore thee !
My daughter lieth at the point of death ;
I pray thee come and lay thy hands upon her,
And she shall live !

CHRISTUS.

Who was it touched my garments ?

SIMON PETER.

Thou seest the multitude that throng and press
    thee,
And sayest thou : Who touched me ? 'T was
    not I.

CHRISTUS.

Some one hath touched my garments ; I perceive
That virtue is gone out of me.

A WOMAN.

O Master !

Forgive me ! For I said within myself,
If I so much as touch his garment's hem,
I shall be whole.

CHRISTUS.

Be of good comfort, daughter !
Thy faith hath made thee whole. Depart in peace.

A MESSENGER *from the house.*

Why troublest thou the Master? Hearest thou not
The flute-players, and the voices of the women
Singing their lamentation? She is dead!

THE MINSTRELS AND MOURNERS.

We have girded ourselves with sackcloth!
We have covered our heads with ashes!
For our young men die, and our maidens
Swoon in the streets of the city;
And into their mother's bosom
They pour out their souls like water!

CHRISTUS, *going in.*

Give place. Why make ye this ado, and weep?
She is not dead, but sleepeth.

THE MOTHER, *from within.*

              Cruel Death!
To take away from me this tender blossom!
To take away my dove, my lamb, my darling!

THE MINSTRELS AND MOURNERS.

He hath led me and brought into darkness,
Like the dead of old in dark places!
He hath bent his bow, and hath set me
Apart as a mark for his arrow!
He hath covered himself with a cloud,
That our prayer should not pass through and reach him!

THE CROWD.

He stands beside her bed !   He takes her hand !
Listen, he speaks to her !

CHRISTUS, *within.*

Maiden, arise !

THE CROWD.

See, she obeys his voice !   She stirs !   She lives !
Her mother holds her folded in her arms !
O miracle of miracles !  O marvel !

## IX.

### THE TOWER OF MAGDALA.

#### MARY MAGDALENE.

COMPANIONLESS, unsatisfied, forlorn,
I sit here in this lonely tower, and look
Upon the lake below me, and the hills
That swoon with heat, and see as in a vision
All my past life unroll itself before me.
The princes and the merchants come to me,
Merchants of Tyre and Princes of Damascus,
And pass, and disappear, and are no more ;
But leave behind their merchandise and jewels,
Their perfumes, and their gold, and their disgust.
I loathe them, and the very memory of them
Is unto me, as thought of food to one

Cloyed with the luscious figs of Dalmanutha!
What if hereafter, in the long hereafter
Of endless joy or pain, or joy in pain,
It were my punishment to be with them
Grown hideous and decrepit in their sins,
And hear them say: Thou that hast brought us
        here,
Be unto us as thou hast been of old!

I look upon this raiment that I wear,
These silks, and these embroideries, and they seem
Only as cerements wrapped about my limbs!
I look upon these rings thick set with pearls,
And emerald and amethyst and jasper,
And they are burning coals upon my flesh!
This serpent on my wrist becomes alive!
Away, thou viper! and away, ye garlands,
Whose odors bring the swift remembrance back
Of the unhallowed revels in these chambers!
But yesterday, — and yet it seems to me
Something remote, like a pathetic song
Sung long ago by minstrels in the street, —
But yesterday, as from this tower I gazed,
Over the olive and the walnut trees
Upon the lake and the white ships, and wondered
Whither and whence they steered, and who was in
        them,
A fisher's boat drew near the landing-place
Under the oleanders, and the people

Came up from it, and passed beneath the tower,
Close under me.   In front of them, as leader,
Walked one of royal aspect, clothed in white,
Who lifted up his eyes, and looked at me,
And all at once the air seemed filled and living
With a mysterious power, that streamed from him,
And overflowed me with an atmosphere
Of light and love.   As one entranced I stood,
And when I woke again, lo! he was gone ;
So that I said : Perhaps it is a dream.
But from that very hour the seven demons
That had their habitation in this body
Which men call beautiful, departed from me !

This morning, when the first gleam of the dawn
Made Lebanon a glory in the air,
And all below was darkness, I beheld
An angel, or a spirit glorified,
With wind-tossed garments walking on the lake.
The face I could not see, but I distinguished
The attitude and gesture, and I knew
'T was he that healed me.   And the gusty wind
Brought to mine ears a voice, which seemed to say :
Be of good cheer !   'T is I !   Be not afraid !
And from the darkness, scarcely heard, the answer :
If it be thou, bid me come unto thee
Upon the water !   And the voice said : Come !
And then I heard a cry of fear : Lord, save me !
As of a drowning man.   And then the voice :

Why didst thou doubt, O thou of little faith!
At this all vanished, and the wind was hushed,
And the great sun came up above the hills,
And the swift-flying vapors hid themselves
In caverns among the rocks! O, I must find him
And follow him, and be with him forever!

Thou box of alabaster, in whose walls
The souls of flowers lie pent, the precious balm
And spikenard of Arabian farms, the spirits
Of aromatic herbs, ethereal natures
Nursed by the sun and dew, not all unworthy
To bathe his consecrated feet, whose step
Makes every threshold holy that he crosses ;
Let us go forth upon our pilgrimage,
Thou and I only! Let us search for him
Until we find him, and pour out our souls
Before his feet, till all that 's left of us
Shall be the broken caskets, that once held us!


## X.

### THE HOUSE OF SIMON THE PHARISEE.

#### A GUEST *at table.*

ARE ye deceived? Have any of the Rulers
Believed on him? or do they know indeed
This man to be the very Christ? Howbeit

We know whence this man is, but when the Christ
Shall come, none knoweth whence he is.

### CHRISTUS.

Whereunto shall I liken, then, the men
Of this generation? and what are they like?
They are like children sitting in the markets,
And calling unto one another, saying:
We have piped unto you, and ye have not danced;
We have mourned unto you, and ye have not wept!
This say I unto you, for John the Baptist
Came neither eating bread nor drinking wine;
Ye say he hath a devil. The Son of Man
Eating and drinking cometh, and ye say:
Behold a gluttonous man, and a wine-bibber;
Behold a friend of publicans and sinners!

### A GUEST, *aside to* SIMON.

Who is that woman yonder, gliding in
So silently behind him?

### SIMON.

It is Mary,
Who dwelleth in the Tower of Magdala.

### THE GUEST.

See, how she kneels there weeping, and her tears
Fall on his feet; and her long, golden hair
Waves to and fro and wipes them dry again.
And now she kisses them, and from a box

Of alabaster is anointing them
With precious ointment, filling all the house
With its sweet odor!

SIMON, *aside.*

O, this man, forsooth,
Were he indeed a Prophet, would have known
Who and what manner of woman this may be
That toucheth him! would know she is a sinner!

CHRISTUS.

Simon, somewhat have I to say to thee.

SIMON.

Master, say on.

CHRISTUS.

A certain creditor
Had once two debtors; and the one of them
Owed him five hundred pence; the other, fifty.
They having naught to pay withal, he frankly
Forgave them both.   Now tell me which of them
Will love him most?

SIMON.

He, I suppose, to whom
He most forgave.

CHRISTUS.

Yea, thou hast rightly judged.
Seest thou this woman?   When thine house I
entered,

Thou gavest me no water for my feet,
But she hath washed them with her tears, and wiped
     them
With her own hair!   Thou gavest me no kiss;
This woman hath not ceased, since I came in,
To kiss my feet!   My head with oil didst thou
Anoint not; but this woman hath anointed
My feet with ointment.   Hence I say to thee,
Her sins, which have been many, are forgiven,
For she loved much.

THE GUESTS.

              O, who, then, is this man
That pardoneth also sins without atonement?

CHRISTUS.

Woman, thy faith hath saved thee!   Go in peace!

# THE DIVINE TRAGEDY

## THE SECOND PASSOVER

4

## BEFORE THE GATES OF MACHÆRUS.

### MANAHEM.

WELCOME, O wilderness, and welcome, night
And solitude, and ye swift-flying stars
That drift with golden sands the barren heavens,
Welcome once more ! The Angels of the Wind
Hasten across the desert to receive me ;
And sweeter than men's voices are to me
The voices of these solitudes ; the sound
Of unseen rivulets, and the far-off cry
Of bitterns in the reeds of water-pools.
And lo! above me, like the Prophet's arrow
Shot from the eastern window, high in air
The clamorous cranes go singing through the night.
O ye mysterious pilgrims of the air,
Would I had wings that I might follow you!

I look forth from these mountains, and behold
The omnipotent and omnipresent night,
Mysterious as the future and the fate
That hangs o'er all men's lives ! I see beneath me
The desert stretching to the Dead Sea shore,
And westward, faint and far away, the glimmer
Of torches on Mount Olivet, announcing

The rising of the Moon of Passover.
Like a great cross it seems, on which suspended,
With head bowed down in agony, I see
A human figure !   Hide, O merciful heaven,
The awful apparition from my sight !

And thou, Machærus, lifting high and black
Thy dreadful walls against the rising moon,
Haunted by demons and by apparitions,
Lilith, and Jezerhara, and Bedargon,
How grim thou showest in the uncertain light,
A palace and a prison, where King Herod
Feasts with Herodias, while the Baptist John
Fasts, and consumes his unavailing life !
And in thy court-yard grows the untithed rue,
Huge as the olives of Gethsemane,
And ancient as the terebinth of Hebron,
Coeval with the world.   Would that its leaves
Medicinal could purge thee of the demons,
That now possess thee, and the cunning fox
That burrows in thy walls, contriving mischief!

*Music is heard from within.*

Angels of God !   Sandalphon, thou that weavest
The prayers of men into immortal garlands,
And thou, Metatron, who dost gather up
Their songs, and bear them to the gates of heaven,
Now gather up together in your hands
The prayers that fill this prison, and the songs

That echo from the ceiling of this palace,
And lay them side by side before God's feet!

*He enters the castle.*

## II.

### HEROD'S BANQUET-HALL.

###### MANAHEM.

Thou hast sent for me, O King, and I am here.

###### HEROD.

Who art thou?

###### MANAHEM.

Manahem, the Essenian.

###### HEROD.

I recognize thy features, but what mean
These torn and faded garments? On thy road
Have demons crowded thee, and rubbed against
    thee,
And given thee weary knees? A cup of wine!

###### MANAHEM.

The Essenians drink no wine.

###### HEROD.

               What wilt thou, then?

###### MANAHEM.

Nothing.

HEROD.

Not even a cup of water?

MANAHEM.

Nothing.

Why hast thou sent for me?

HEROD.

Dost thou remember
One day when I, a schoolboy in the streets
Of the great city, met thee on my way
To school, and thou didst say to me: Hereafter
Thou shalt be King?

MANAHEM.

Yea, I remember it.

HEROD.

Thinking thou didst not know me, I replied:
I am of humble birth; whereat, thou, smiling,
Didst smite me with thy hand, and saidst again:
Thou shalt be King; and let the friendly blows
That Manahem hath given thee on this day
Remind thee of the fickleness of fortune.

MANAHEM.

What more?

HEROD.

No more.

MANAHEM.

                    Yea, for I said to thee :
It shall be well with thee if thou love justice
And clemency towards thy fellow-men.
Hast thou done this, O King?

HEROD.

                    Go, ask my people.

MANAHEM.

And then, foreseeing all thy life, I added :
But these thou wilt forget ; and at the end
Of life the Lord will punish thee.

HEROD.

                    The end !
When will that come ?   For this I sent to thee.
How long shall I still reign?   Thou dost not
        answer!
Speak ! shall I reign ten years?

MANAHEM.

                    Thou shalt reign twenty,
Nay, thirty years.   I cannot name the end.

HEROD.

Thirty ?   I thank thee, good Essenian !
This is my birthday, and a happier one
Was never mine.   We hold a banquet here.
See, yonder are Herodias and her daughter.

MANAHEM, *aside.*

'T is said that devils sometimes take the shape
Of ministering angels, clothed with air,
That they may be inhabitants of earth,
And lead man to destruction.   Such are these.

HEROD.

Knowest thou John the Baptist?

MANAHEM.

                              Yea, I know him ;
Who knows him not?

HEROD.

                        Know, then, this John the Baptist
Said that it was not lawful I should marry
My brother Philip's wife, and John the Baptist
Is here in prison.   In my father's time
Matthias Margaloth was put to death
For tearing the golden eagle from its station
Above the Temple Gate, — a slighter crime
Than John is guilty of.   These things are warnings
To intermeddlers not to play with eagles,
Living or dead.   I think the Essenians
Are wiser, or more wary, are they not?

MANAHEM.

The Essenians do not marry.

HEROD.

                    Thou hast given
My words a meaning foreign to my thought.

MANAHEM.

Let me go hence, O King!

HEROD.

                    Stay yet awhile,
And see the daughter of Herodias dance.
Cleopatra of Jerusalem, my mother,
In her best days, was not more beautiful.

*Music.* THE DAUGHTER OF HERODIAS *dances.*

HEROD.

O, what was Miriam dancing with her timbrel,
Compared to this one?

MANAHEM, *aside.*

                  O thou Angel of Death,
Dancing at funerals among the women,
When men bear out the dead! The air is hot
And stifles me! O for a breath of air!
Bid me depart, O King!

HEROD.

                  Not yet. Come hither,
Salome, thou enchantress! Ask of me
Whate'er thou wilt; and even unto the half
Of all my kingdom, I will give it thee,
As the Lord liveth!

DAUGHTER OF HERODIAS, *kneeling.*

                    Give me here the head
Of John the Baptist on this silver charger !

HEROD.

Not that, dear child !   I dare not ; for the people
Regard John as a prophet.

DAUGHTER OF HERODIAS.

                    Thou hast sworn it.

HEROD.

For mine oath's sake, then.   Send unto the prison ;
Let him die quickly.   O accursed oath !

MANAHEM.

Bid me depart, O King !

HEROD.

                    Good Manahem,
Give me thy hand.   I love the Essenians.
He 's gone and hears me not !   The guests are
        dumb,
Awaiting the pale face, the silent witness.
The lamps flare ; and the curtains of the doorways
Wave to and fro as if a ghost were passing !
Strengthen my heart, red wine of Ascalon !

# III.

## UNDER THE WALLS OF MACHÆRUS.

MANAHEM, *rushing out.*

Away from this Palace of sin !
The demons, the terrible powers
Of the air, that haunt its towers
And hide in its water-spouts,
Deafen me with the din
Of their laughter and their shouts
For the crimes that are done within !

Sink back into the earth,
Or vanish into the air,
Thou castle of despair !
Let it all be but a dream
Of the things of monstrous birth,
Of the things that only seem !
White Angel of the Moon,
Onafiel ! be my guide
Out of this hateful place
Of sin and death, nor hide
In yon black cloud too soon
Thy pale and tranquil face !

*A trumpet is blown from the walls.*

Hark ! hark ! It is the breath
Of the trump of doom and death,
From the battlements overhead

Like a burden of sorrow cast
On the midnight and the blast,
A wailing for the dead,
That the gusts drop and uplift !
O Herod, thy vengeance is swift !
O Herodias, thou hast been
The demon, the evil thing,
That in place of Esther the Queen,
In place of the lawful bride,
Hast lain at night by the side
Of Ahasuerus the king !

*The trumpet again.*

The Prophet of God is dead !
At a drunken monarch's call,
At a dancing-woman's beck,
They have severed that stubborn neck,
And into the banquet-hall
Are bearing the ghastly head !

*A body is thrown from the tower.*

A torch of lurid red
Lights the window with its glow ;
And a white mass as of snow
Is hurled into the abyss
Of the black precipice,
That yawns for it below !
O hand of the Most High,
O hand of Adonai !
Bury it, hide it away
From the birds and beasts of prey,

And the eyes of the homicide,
More pitiless than they,
As thou didst bury of yore
The body of him that died
On the mountain of Peor!

Even now I behold a sign,
A threatening of wrath divine,
A watery, wandering star,
Through whose streaming hair, and the white
Unfolding garments of light,
That trail behind it afar,
The constellations shine!
And the whiteness and brightness appear
Like the Angel bearing the Seer
By the hair of his head, in the might
And rush of his vehement flight.
And I listen until I hear
From fathomless depths of the sky
The voice of his prophecy
Sounding louder and more near!

Malediction! malediction!
May the lightnings of heaven fall
On palace and prison wall,
And their desolation be
As the day of fear and affliction,
As the day of anguish and ire,
With the burning and fuel of fire,
In the Valley of the Sea!

## IV.

### NICODEMUS AT NIGHT.

#### NICODEMUS.

THE streets are silent.   The dark houses seem
Like sepulchres, in which the sleepers lie
Wrapped in their shrouds, and for the moment
          dead.
The lamps are all extinguished ; only one
Burns steadily, and from the door its light
Lies like a shining gate across the street.
He waits for me.   Ah, should this be at last
The long-expected Christ !   I see him there
Sitting alone, deep-buried in his thought,
As if the weight of all the world were resting
Upon him, and thus bowed him down.   O Rabbi,
We know thou art a Teacher come from God,
For no man can perform the miracles
Thou dost perform, except the Lord be with him.
Thou art a Prophet, sent here to proclaim
The Kingdom of the Lord.   Behold in me
A Ruler of the Jews, who long have waited
The coming of that kingdom.   Tell me of it.

#### CHRISTUS.

Verily, verily I say unto thee,
Except a man be born again, he cannot
Behold the Kingdom of God !

NICODEMUS.

> Be born again?
How can a man be born when he is old?
Say, can he enter for a second time
Into his mother's womb, and so be born?

CHRISTUS.

Verily I say unto thee, except
A man be born of water and the spirit,
He cannot enter into the Kingdom of God.
For that which of the flesh is born, is flesh;
And that which of the spirit is born, is spirit.

NICODEMUS.

We Israelites from the Primeval Man
Adam Ahelion derive our bodies;
Our souls are breathings of the Holy Ghost.
No more than this we know, or need to know.

CHRISTUS.

Then marvel not, that I said unto thee
Ye must be born again.

NICODEMUS.

> The mystery
Of birth and death we cannot comprehend.

CHRISTUS.

The wind bloweth where it listeth, and we hear
The sound thereof, but know not whence it cometh,

Nor whither it goeth.   So is every one
Born of the spirit !

NICODEMUS, *aside.*

How can these things be ?
He seems to speak of some vague realm of shadows,
Some unsubstantial kingdom of the air !
It is not this the Jews are waiting for,
Nor can this be the Christ, the Son of David,
Who shall deliver us !

CHRISTUS.

Art thou a master
Of Israel, and knowest not these things ?
We speak that we do know, and testify
That we have seen, and ye will not receive
Our witness.   If I tell you earthly things,
And ye believe not, how shall ye believe,
If I should tell you of things heavenly ?
And no man hath ascended up to heaven,
But he alone that first came down from heaven,
Even the Son of Man which is in heaven !

NICODEMUS, *aside.*

This is a dreamer of dreams ; a visionary,
Whose brain is overtasked, until he deems
The unseen world to be a thing substantial,
And this we live in an unreal vision !
And yet his presence fascinates and fills me

With wonder, and I feel myself exalted
Into a higher region, and become
Myself in part a dreamer of his dreams,
A seer of his visions!

CHRISTUS.

And as Moses
Uplifted the serpent in the wilderness,
So must the Son of Man be lifted up ;
That whosoever shall believe in him
Shall perish not, but have eternal life.
He that believes in him is not condemned ;
He that believes not, is condemned already.

NICODEMUS, *aside.*

He speaketh like a Prophet of the Lord!

CHRISTUS.

This is the condemnation ; that the light
Is come into the world, and men loved darkness
Rather than light, because their deeds are evil!

NICODEMUS, *aside.*

Of me he speaketh! He reproveth me,
Because I come by night to question him!

CHRISTUS.

For every one that doeth evil deeds
Hateth the light, nor cometh to the light,
Lest he should be reproved.

5

NICODEMUS, *aside.*

Alas, how truly
He readeth what is passing in my heart!

CHRISTUS.

But he that doeth truth comes to the light,
So that his deeds may be made manifest,
That they are wrought in God.

NICODEMUS.

Alas! alas!

## V.

### BLIND BARTIMEUS.

BARTIMEUS.

BE not impatient, Chilion; it is pleasant
To sit here in the shadow of the walls.
Under the palms, and hear the hum of bees,
And rumor of voices passing to and fro,
And drowsy bells of caravans on their way
To Sidon or Damascus.   This is still
The City of Palms, and yet the walls thou seest
Are not the old walls, not the walls where Rahab
Hid the two spies, and let them down by cords
Out of the window, when the gates were shut,
And it was dark.   Those walls were overthrown
When Joshua's army shouted, and the priests
Blew with their seven trumpets.

CHILION.

When was that?

BARTIMEUS.

O, my sweet rose of Jericho, I know not.
Hundreds of years ago.   And over there
Beyond the river, the great prophet Elijah
Was taken by a whirlwind up to heaven
In chariot of fire, with fiery horses.
That is the plain of Moab; and beyond it
Rise the blue summits of Mount Abarim,
Nebo and Pisgah and Peor, where Moses
Died, whom the Lord knew face to face, and whom
He buried in a valley, and no man
Knows of his sepulchre unto this day.

CHILION.

Would thou couldst see these places, as I see them.

BARTIMEUS.

I have not seen a glimmer of the light
Since thou wast born.   I never saw thy face,
And yet I seem to see it; and one day
Perhaps shall see it; for there is a Prophet
In Galilee, the Messiah, the Son of David,
Who heals the blind, if I could only find him.
I hear the sound of many feet approaching
And voices, like the murmur of a crowd!
What seest thou?

CHILION.

A young man clad in white
Is coming through the gateway, and a crowd
Of people follow.

BARTIMEUS.

Can it be the Prophet?
O neighbors, tell me who it is that passes!

ONE OF THE CROWD.

Jesus of Nazareth.

BARTIMEUS, *crying.*

O Son of David!
Have mercy on me!

MANY OF THE CROWD.

Peace, Blind Bartimeus!
Do not disturb the Master.

BARTIMEUS, *crying more vehemently.*

Son of David,
Have mercy on me!

ONE OF THE CROWD.

See, the Master stops.
Be of good comfort; rise, he calleth thee!

BARTIMEUS, *casting away his cloak.*

Chilion! good neighbors! lead me on.

CHRISTUS.

What wilt thou
That I should do to thee?

BARTIMEUS.

Good Lord! my sight —
That I receive my sight!

CHRISTUS.

Receive thy sight!
Thy faith hath made thee whole!

THE CROWD.

He sees again!

CHRISTUS *passes on.  The crowd gathers round* BARTIMEUS.

BARTIMEUS.

I see again; but sight bewilders me!
Like a remembered dream, familiar things
Come back to me.  I see the tender sky
Above me, see the trees, the city walls,
And the old gateway, through whose echoing arch
I groped so many years; and you, my neighbors;
But know you by your friendly voices only.
How beautiful the world is! and how wide!
O, I am miles away, if I but look!
Where art thou, Chilion?

CHILION.

Father, I am here.

BARTIMEUS.

O let me gaze upon thy face, dear child!
For I have only seen thee with my hands!
How beautiful thou art! I should have known thee;
Thou hast her eyes whom we shall see hereafter!
O God of Abraham! Elion! Adonai!
Who art thyself a Father, pardon me
If for a moment I have thee postponed
To the affections and the thoughts of earth,
Thee, and the adoration that I owe thee,
When by thy power alone these darkened eyes
Have been unsealed again to see thy light!


## VI.

### JACOB'S WELL.

A SAMARITAN WOMAN.

THE sun is hot; and the dry east-wind blowing
Fills all the air with dust. The birds are silent;
Even the little fieldfares in the corn
No longer twitter; only the grasshoppers
Sing their incessant song of sun and summer.
I wonder who those strangers were I met
Going into the city? Galileans
They seemed to me in speaking, when they asked
The short way to the market-place. Perhaps
They are fishermen from the lake; or travellers,
Looking to find the inn. And here is some one

Sitting beside the well; another stranger;
A Galilean also by his looks.
What can so many Jews be doing here
Together in Samaria?   Are they going
Up to Jerusalem to the Passover?
Our Passover is better here at Sychem,
For here is Ebal; here is Gerizim,
The mountain where our father Abraham
Went up to offer Isaac ; here the tomb
Of Joseph, — for they brought his bones from
     Egypt
And buried them in this land, and it is holy.

#### CHRISTUS.

Give me to drink.

#### SAMARITAN WOMAN.

       How can it be that thou,
Being a Jew, askest to drink of me
Which am a woman of Samaria?
You Jews despise us ; have no dealings with us ;
Make us a byword ; call us in derision
The silly folk of Sychar.   Sir, how is it
Thou askest drink of me?

#### CHRISTUS.

       If thou hadst known
The gift of God, and who it is that sayeth
Give me to drink, thou wouldst have asked of him ;
He would have given thee the living water.

### SAMARITAN WOMAN.

Sir, thou hast naught to draw with, and the well
Is deep ! Whence hast thou living water ?
Say, art thou greater than our father Jacob,
Which gave this well to us, and drank thereof
Himself, and all his children and his cattle ?

### CHRISTUS.

Ah, whosoever drinketh of this water
Shall thirst again ; but whosocvcr drinkcth
The water I shall give him shall not thirst
Forevermore, for it shall be within him
A well of living water, springing up
Into life everlasting.

### SAMARITAN WOMAN.

Every day
I must go to and fro, in heat and cold,
And I am weary. Give me of this water,
That I may thirst not, nor come here to draw.

### CHRISTUS.

Go call thy husband, woman, and come hither.

### SAMARITAN WOMAN.

I have no husband, Sir.

### CHRISTUS.

Thou hast well said
I have no husband. Thou hast had five husbands;
And he whom now thou hast is not thy husband.

SAMARITAN WOMAN.

Surely thou art a Prophet, for thou readest
The hidden things of life ! Our fathers worshipped
Upon this mountain Gerizim ; and ye say
The only place in which men ought to worship
Is at Jerusalem.

CHRISTUS.

Believe me, woman,
The hour is coming, when ye neither shall
Upon this mount, nor at Jerusalem,
Worship the Father ; for the hour is coming,
And is now come, when the true worshippers
Shall worship the Father in spirit and in truth !
The Father seeketh such to worship him.
God is a spirit ; and they that worship him
Must worship him in spirit and in truth.

SAMARITAN WOMAN.

Master, I know that the Messiah cometh,
Which is called Christ ; and he will tell us all things.

CHRISTUS.

I that speak unto thee am he !

THE DISCIPLES, *returning*.

Behold,
The Master sitting by the well, and talking
With a Samaritan woman ! With a woman

Of Sychar, the silly people, always boasting
Of their Mount Ebal, and Mount Gerizim,
Their Everlasting Mountain, which they think
Higher and holier than our Mount Moriah!
Why, once upon the Feast of the New Moon,
When our great Sanhedrim of Jerusalem
Had all its watch-fires kindled on the hills
To warn the distant villages, these people
Lighted up others to mislead the Jews,
And make a mockery of their festival!
See, she has left the Master ; and is running
Back to the city!

THE SAMARITAN WOMAN.

O, come see a man
Who hath told me all things that I ever did!
Say, is not this the Christ?

THE DISCIPLES.

Lo, Master, here
Is food, that we have brought thee from the city.
We pray thee eat it.

CHRISTUS.

I have food to eat
Ye know not of.

THE DISCIPLES, *to each other.*

Hath any man been here,
And brought him aught to eat, while we were gone?

CHRISTUS.

The food I speak of is to do the will
Of him that sent me, and to finish his work.
Do ye not say, Lo ! there are yet four months
And cometh harvest ?   I say unto you,
Lift up your eyes, and look upon the fields,
For they are white already unto harvest !


VII.

THE COASTS OF CÆSAREA PHILIPPI.

CHRISTUS, *going up the mountain.*

WHO do the people say I am ?

JOHN.
                        Some say
That thou art John the Baptist ; some, Elias ;
And others Jeremiah.

JAMES.
                  Or that one
Of the old Prophets is arisen again.

CHRISTUS.

But who say ye I am ?

PETER.
                        Thou art the Christ !
Thou art the Son of God !

CHRISTUS.

                    Blessed art thou,
Simon Barjona! Flesh and blood hath not
Revealed it unto thee, but even my Father,
Which is in Heaven. And I say unto thee
That thou art Peter; and upon this rock
I build my Church, and all the gates of Hell
Shall not prevail against it. But take heed
Ye tell to no man that I am the Christ.
For I must go up to Jerusalem,
And suffer many things, and be rejected
Of the Chief Priests, and of the Scribes and Elders,
And must be crucified, and the third day
Shall rise again!

PETER.

                    Be it far from thee, Lord!
This shall not be!

CHRISTUS.

                    Get thee behind me, Satan!
Thou savorest not the things that be of God,
But those that be of men! If any will
Come after me, let him deny himself,
And daily take his cross, and follow me.
For whosoever will save his life shall lose it,
And whosoever will lose his life shall find it.
For wherein shall a man be profited
If he shall gain the whole world, and shall lose
Himself or be a castaway?

JAMES, *after a long pause.*

> Why doth
> The Master lead us up into this mountain?

PETER.

He goeth up to pray.

JOHN.

> See, where he standeth
> Above us on the summit of the hill!
> His face shines as the sun! and all his raiment
> Exceeding white as snow, so as no fuller
> On earth can white them! He is not alone;
> There are two with him there; two men of eld,
> Their white beards blowing on the mountain air,
> Are talking with him.

JAMES.

> I am sore afraid!

PETER.

Who and whence are they?

JOHN.

> Moses and Elias!

PETER.

O Master! it is good for us to be here!
If thou wilt, let us make three tabernacles;
For thee one, and for Moses and Elias!

JOHN.

Behold a bright cloud sailing in the sun !
It overshadows us.   A golden mist
Now hides them from us, and envelops us
And all the mountain in a luminous shadow !
I see no more.   The nearest rocks are hidden.

VOICE *from the cloud.*

Lo ! this is my beloved Son !   Hear him !

PETER.

It is the voice of God.   He speaketh to us,
As from the burning bush he spake to Moses !

JOHN.

The cloud-wreaths roll away.   The veil is lifted ;
We see again.   Behold ! he is alone.
It was a vision that our eyes beheld,
And it hath vanished into the unseen.

CHRISTUS, *coming down from the mountain.*

I charge ye, tell the vision unto no one,
Till the Son of Man be risen from the dead !

PETER, *aside.*

Again he speaks of it !   What can it mean,
This rising from the dead ?

JAMES.

                Why say the Scribes
Elias must first come ?

CHRISTUS.

He cometh first,
Restoring all things.    But I say to you,
That this Elias is already come.           .
They knew him not, but have done unto him
Whate'er they listed, as is written of him.

PETER, *aside.*

It is of John the Baptist he is speaking.

JAMES.

As we descend, see, at the mountain's foot,
A crowd of people ; coming, going, thronging
Round the disciples, that we left behind us,
Seeming impatient, that we stay so long.

PETER.

It is some blind man, or some paralytic
That waits the Master's coming to be healed.

JAMES.

I see a boy, who struggles and demeans him
As if an unclean spirit tormented him !

A CERTAIN MAN, *running forward.*

Lord ! I beseech thee, look upon my son.
He is mine only child ; a lunatic,
And sorely vexed ; for oftentimes he falleth
Into the fire and oft into the water.

Wherever the dumb spirit taketh him
He teareth him.   He gnasheth with his teeth,
And pines away.   I spake to thy disciples
That they should cast him out, and they could not.

CHRISTUS.

O faithless generation and perverse!
How long shall I be with you, and suffer you?
Bring thy son hither.

BYSTANDERS.

How the unclean spirit
Seizes the boy, and tortures him with pain!
He falleth to the ground and wallows, foaming!
He cannot live.

CHRISTUS.

How long is it ago
Since this came unto him?

THE FATHER.

Even of a child.
O have compassion on us, Lord, and help us,
If thou canst help us.

CHRISTUS.

If thou canst believe!
For unto him that verily believeth,
All things are possible.

THE FATHER.
                        Lord, I believe!
Help thou mine unbelief!

CHRISTUS.
                        Dumb and deaf spirit,
Come out of him, I charge thee, and no more
Enter thou into him!

*The boy utters a loud cry of pain, and then lies still.*

BYSTANDERS.
                        How motionless
He lieth there.   No life is left in him.
His eyes are like a blind man's, that see not.
The boy is dead!

OTHERS.
                        Behold! the Master stoops,
And takes him by the hand, and lifts him up.
He is not dead.

DISCIPLES.
                        But one word from those lips,
But one touch of that hand, and he is healed!
Ah, why could we not do it?

THE FATHER.
                        My poor child!
Now thou art mine again.   The unclean spirit
Shall never more torment thee!   Look at me!
Speak unto me!   Say that thou knowest me!

6

DISCIPLES *to* CHRISTUS, *departing.*

Good Master, tell us, for what reason was it
We could not cast him out?

CHRISTUS.

Because of your unbelief!

## VIII.

### THE YOUNG RULER.

CHRISTUS.

Two men went up into the temple to pray.
The one was a self-righteous Pharisee,
The other a Publican. And the Pharisee
Stood and prayed thus within himself: O God,
I thank thee I am not as other men,
Extortioners, unjust, adulterers,
Or even as this Publican. I fast
Twice in the week, and also I give tithes
Of all that I possess! The Publican,
Standing afar off, would not lift so much
Even as his eyes to heaven, but smote his breast,
Saying: God be merciful to me a sinner!
I tell you that this man went to his house
More justified than the other. Every one
That doth exalt himself shall be abased,
And he that humbleth himself shall be exalted!

CHILDREN, *among themselves.*

Let us go nearer!   He is telling stories!
Let us go listen to them.

AN OLD JEW.

Children, children!
What are ye doing here?   Why do ye crowd us?
It was such little vagabonds as you,
That followed Elisha, mocking him and crying:
Go up, thou bald-head!   But the bears — the bears
Came out of the wood, and tare them!

A MOTHER.

Speak not thus!
We brought them here, that he might lay his hands
On them, and bless them.

CHRISTUS.

Suffer little children
To come unto me, and forbid them not;
Of such is the kingdom of heaven; and their angels
Look always on my Father's face.

*Takes them in his arms and blesses them.*

A YOUNG RULER, *running.*

Good Master!
What good thing shall I do, that I may have
Eternal life?

CHRISTUS.

Why callest thou me good?
There is none good but one, and that is God.

If thou wilt enter into life eternal,
Keep the commandments.

### YOUNG RULER.

Which of them?

### CHRISTUS.

Thou shalt not
Commit adultery; thou shalt not kill;
Thou shalt not steal; thou shalt not bear false
    witness;
Honor thy father and thy mother; and love
Thy neighbor as thyself.

### YOUNG RULER.

From my youth up
All these things have I kept.    What lack I yet?

### JOHN.

With what divine compassion in his eyes
The Master looks upon this eager youth,
As if he loved him!

### CHRISTUS.

Wouldst thou perfect be,
Sell all thou hast, and give it to the poor,
And come, take up thy cross, and follow me,
And thou shalt have thy treasure in the heavens.

### JOHN.

Behold, how sorrowful he turns away!

#### CHRISTUS.

Children! how hard it is for them that trust
In riches to enter into the kingdom of God!
'T is easier for a camel to go through
A needle's eye, than for the rich to enter
The kingdom of God!

#### JOHN.

        Ah, who then can be saved?

#### CHRISTUS.

With men this is indeed impossible,
But unto God all things are possible!

#### PETER.

Behold, we have left all, and followed thee.
What shall we have therefore?

#### CHRISTUS.

        Eternal life.


### IX.

#### AT BETHANY.

MARTHA *busy about household affairs.* MARY *sitting at the feet of* CHRISTUS.

#### MARTHA.

SHE sitteth idly at the Master's feet,
And troubles not herself with household cares.
'T is the old story. When a guest arrives

She gives up all to be with him ; while I
Must be the drudge, make ready the guest-chamber,
Prepare the food, set everything in order,
And see that naught is wanting in the house.
She shows her love by words, and I by works.

MARY.

O Master ! when thou comest, it is always
A Sabbath in the house.   I cannot work ;
I must sit at thy feet ; must see thee, hear thee !
I have a feeble, wayward, doubting heart,
Incapable of endurance or great thoughts,
Striving for something that it cannot reach,
Baffled and disappointed, wounded, hungry ;
And only when I hear thee am I happy,
And only when I see thee am at peace !

Stronger than I, and wiser, and far better
In every manner, is my sister Martha.
You see how well she orders everything
To make thee welcome ; how she comes and goes,
Careful and cumbered ever with much serving,
While I but welcome thee with foolish words !
Whene'er thou speakest to me, I am happy ;
When thou art silent, I am satisfied.
Thy presence is enough.   I ask no more.
Only to be with thee, only to see thee,
Sufficeth me.   My heart is then at rest.
I wonder I am worthy of so much.

### MARTHA.

Lord, dost thou care not that my sister Mary
Hath left me thus to wait on thee alone?
I pray thee, bid her help me.

### CHRISTUS.

                    Martha, Martha,
Careful and troubled about many things
Art thou, and yet one thing alone is needful!
Thy sister Mary hath chosen that good part,
Which never shall be taken away from her!

## X.

### BORN BLIND.

### A JEW.

Who is this beggar blinking in the sun?
Is it not he who used to sit and beg
By the Gate Beautiful?

### ANOTHER.

                 It is the same.

### A THIRD.

It is not he, but like him, for that beggar
Was blind from birth.   It cannot be the same.

THE BEGGAR.

Yea, I am he.

A JEW.

How have thine eyes been opened?

THE BEGGAR.

A man that is called Jesus made a clay
And put it on mine eyes, and said to me:
Go to Siloam's Pool and wash thyself.
I went and washed, and I received my sight.

A JEW.

Where is he?

THE BEGGAR.

I know not.

PHARISEES.

What is this crowd
Gathered about a beggar?   What has happened?

A JEW.

Here is a man who hath been blind from birth,
And now he sees.   He says a man called Jesus
Hath healed him.

PHARISEES.

As God liveth, the Nazarene!
How was this done?

THE BEGGAR.

Rabboni, he put clay
Upon mine eyes; I washed, and now I see.

PHARISEES.

When did he this?

THE BEGGAR.

Rabboni, yesterday.

PHARISEES.

The Sabbath-day.   This man is not of God
Because he keepeth not the Sabbath-day!

A JEW.

How can a man that is a sinner do
Such miracles?

PHARISEES.

What dost thou say of him
That hath restored thy sight?

THE BEGGAR.

He is a Prophet.

A JEW.

This is a wonderful story, but not true.
A beggar's fiction.   He was not born blind,
And never has been blind!

OTHERS.

Here are his parents.
Ask them.

PHARISEES.

Is this your son ?

THE PARENTS.

Rabboni, yea ;
We know this is our son.

PHARISEES.

Was he born blind ?

THE PARENTS.

He was born blind.

PHARISEES.

Then how doth he now see ?

THE PARENTS, *aside.*

What answer shall we make ?   If we confess
It was the Christ, we shall be driven forth
Out of the Synagogue !   We know, Rabboni,
This is our son, and that he was born blind ;
But by what means he seeth, we know not,
Or who his eyes hath opened, we know not.
He is of age ; ask him ; we cannot say ;
He shall speak for himself.

PHARISEES.

Give God the praise!
We know the man that healed thee is a sinner!

THE BEGGAR.

Whether he be a sinner, I know not;
One thing I know; that whereas I was blind,
I now do see.

PHARISEES.

How opened he thine eyes?
What did he do?

THE BEGGAR.

I have already told you.
Ye did not hear; why would ye hear again?
Will ye be his disciples?

PHARISEES.

God of Moses!
Are we demoniacs, are we halt or blind,
Or palsy-stricken, or lepers, or the like,
That we should join the Synagogue of Satan,
And follow jugglers? Thou art his disciple,
But we are disciples of Moses; and we know
That God spake unto Moses; but this fellow,
We know not whence he is!

THE BEGGAR.

Why, herein is
A marvellous thing! Ye know not whence he is,

Yet he hath opened mine eyes! We know that
    God
Heareth not sinners ; but if any man
Doeth God's will, and is his worshipper,
Him doth he hear. O, since the world began
It was not heard that any man hath opened
The eyes of one that was born blind. If he
Were not of God, surely he could do nothing!

#### PHARISEES.

Thou, who wast altogether born in sins
And in iniquities, dost thou teach us?
Away with thee out of the holy places,
Thou reprobate, thou beggar, thou blasphemer!

        THE BEGGAR *is cast out.*

## XI.

### SIMON MAGUS AND HELEN OF TYRE.

*On the house-top at Endor. Night. A lighted lantern on a
table.*

#### SIMON.

SWIFT are the blessed Immortals to the mortal
That perseveres! So doth it stand recorded
In the divine Chaldæan Oracles
Of Zoroaster, once Ezekiel's slave,
Who in his native East betook himself

To lonely meditation, and the writing
On the dried skins of oxen the Twelve Books
Of the Avesta and the Oracles !
Therefore I persevere ; and I have brought thee
From the great city of Tyre, where men deride
The things they comprehend not, to this plain
Of Esdraelon, in the Hebrew tongue
Called Armageddon, and this town of Endor,
Where men believe ; where all the air is full
Of marvellous traditions, and the Enchantress
That summoned up the ghost of Samuel,
Is still remembered.   Thou hast seen the land ;
Is it not fair to look on ?


HELEN.

                    It is fair,
Yet not so fair as Tyre.


SIMON.

                    Is not Mount Tabor
As beautiful as Carmel by the Sea ?


HELEN.

It is too silent and too solitary ;
I miss the tumult of the streets ; the sounds
Of traffic, and the going to and fro
Of people in gay attire, with cloaks of purple,
And gold and silver jewelry !

SIMON.

Inventions
Of Ahriman, the spirit of the dark,
The Evil Spirit!

HELEN.

I regret the gossip
Of friends and neighbors at the open door
On summer nights.

SIMON.

An idle waste of time.

HELEN.

The singing and the dancing, the delight
Of music and of motion.   Woe is me,
To give up all these pleasures, and to lead
The life we lead!

SIMON.

Thou canst not raise thyself
Up to the level of my higher thought,
And though possessing thee, I still remain
Apart from thee, and with thee, am alone
In my high dreams.

HELEN.

Happier was I in Tyre.
O, I remember how the gallant ships
Came sailing in, with ivory, gold and silver,
And apes and peacocks; and the singing sailors;
And the gay captains with their silken dresses,
Smelling of aloes, myrrh, and cinnamon!

SIMON.

But the dishonor, Helen! Let the ships
Of Tarshish howl for that!


HELEN.

                        And what dishonor?
Remember Rahab, and how she became
The ancestress of the great Psalmist David ;
And wherefore should not I, Helen of Tyre,
Attain like honor?


SIMON.

                        Thou art Helen of Tyre,
And hast been Helen of Troy, and hast been
        Rahab,
The Queen of Sheba, and Semiramis,
And Sara of seven husbands, and Jezebel,
And other women of the like allurements ;
And now thou art Minerva, the first Æon,
The Mother of Angels!


HELEN.

                        And the concubine
Of Simon the Magician! Is it honor
For one who has been all these noble dames,
To tramp about the dirty villages
And cities of Samaria with a juggler?
A charmer of serpents?

SIMON.

He who knows himself
Knows all things in himself. I have charmed thee,
Thou beautiful asp ; yet am I no magician.
I am the Power of God, and the Beauty of God !
I am the Paraclete, the Comforter !

HELEN.

Illusions ! Thou deceiver, self-deceived !
Thou dost usurp the titles of another ;
Thou art not what thou sayest.

SIMON.

Am I not ?
Then feel my power.

HELEN.

Would I had ne'er left Tyre !

*He looks at her, and she sinks into a deep sleep.*

SIMON.

Go, see it in thy dreams, fair unbeliever !
And leave me unto mine, if they be dreams,
That take such shapes before me, that I see them ;
These effable and ineffable impressions
Of the mysterious world, that come to me
From the elements of Fire and Earth and Water,
And the all-nourishing Ether ! It is written,
Look not on Nature, for her name is fatal !
Yet there are Principles, that make apparent

The images of unapparent things,
And the impression of vague characters
And visions most divine appear in ether.
So speak the Oracles ; then wherefore fatal ?
I take this orange-bough, with its five leaves,
Each equidistant on the upright stem ;
And I project them on a plane below,
In the circumference of a circle drawn
About a centre where the stem is planted,
And each still equidistant from the other ;
As if a thread of gossamer were drawn
Down from each leaf, and fastened with a pin.
Now if from these five points a line be traced
To each alternate point, we shall attain
The Pentagram, or Solomon's Pentangle,
A charm against all witchcraft, and a sign,
Which on the banner of Antiochus
Drove back the fierce barbarians of the North,
Demons esteemed, and gave the Syrian King
The sacred name of Soter, or of Savior.
Thus Nature works mysteriously with man ;
And from the Eternal One, as from a centre,
All things proceed, in fire, air, earth, and water,
And all are subject to one law, which broken
Even in a single point, is broken in all ;
Demons rush in, and chaos comes again.

By this will I compel the stubborn spirits,
That guard the treasures, hid in caverns deep

On Gerizim, by Uzzi the High-Priest,
The ark and holy vessels, to reveal
Their secret unto me, and to restore
These precious things to the Samaritans.

A mist is rising from the plain below me,
And as I look, the vapors shape themselves
Into strange figures, as if unawares
My lips had breathed the Tetragrammaton,
And from their graves, o'er all the battle-fields
Of Armageddon, the long-buried captains
Had started, with their thousands, and ten thou-
        sands,
And rushed together to renew their wars,
Powerless, and weaponless, and without a sound !
Wake, Helen, from thy sleep !   The air grows cold ;
Let us go down.

HELEN, *awaking.*

O would I were at home !

SIMON.

Thou sayest that I usurp another's titles.
In youth I saw the Wise Men of the East,
Magalath and Pangalath, and Saracen,
Who followed the bright star, but home returned
For fear of Herod by another way.
O shining worlds above me ! in what deep
Recesses of your realms of mystery

Lies hidden now that star? and where are they
That brought the gifts of frankincense and myrrh?

#### HELEN.

The Nazarene still liveth.

#### SIMON.

We have heard
His name in many towns, but have not seen him.
He flits before us; tarries not; is gone
When we approach, like something unsubstantial,
Made of the air, and fading into air.
He is at Nazareth, he is at Nain,
Or at the Lovely Village on the Lake,
Or sailing on its waters.

#### HELEN.

So say those
Who do not wish to find him.

#### SIMON.

Can this be
The King of Israel, whom the Wise Men wor-
shipped?
Or does he fear to meet me? It would seem so.
We should soon learn which of us twain usurps
The titles of the other, as thou sayest.

*They go down.*

# THE DIVINE TRAGEDY

## THE THIRD PASSOVER

# I.

## THE ENTRY INTO JERUSALEM.

### THE DAUGHTER, *singing.*

BLIND Bartimeus at the gates
    Of Jericho in darkness waits;
He hears the crowd; — he hears a breath
Say: It is Christ of Nazareth!
And calls, in tones of agony,
Ἰησοῦ, ἐλέησόν με !

The thronging multitudes increase;
Blind Bartimeus, hold thy peace!
But still, above the noisy crowd,
The beggar's cry is shrill and loud;
Until they say: He calleth thee!
Θάρσει, ἔγειραι, φωνεῖ σε !

Then saith the Christ, as silent stands
The crowd: What wilt thou at my hands?
And he replies: O, give me light!
Rabbi, restore the blind man's sight!
And Jesus answers, Ὕπαγε ·
Ἡ πίστις σου σέσωκέ σε !

Ye that have eyes, yet cannot see,
In darkness and in misery,

Recall those mighty voices Three,
᾿Ιησοῦ, ἐλέησόν με!
Θάρσει, ἔγειραι, Ὕπαγε!
῾Η πίστις σου σέσωκέ σε!


### THE MOTHER.

Thy faith hath saved thee! Ah, how true that is!
For I had faith; and when the Master came
Into the coasts of Tyre and Sidon, fleeing
From those who sought to slay him, I went forth
And cried unto him, saying: Have mercy on me,
O Lord, thou Son of David! for my daughter
Is grievously tormented with a devil.
But he passed on, and answered not a word.
And his disciples said, beseeching him:
Send her away! She crieth after us!
And then the Master answered them and said:
I am not sent but unto the lost sheep
Of the House of Israel! Then I worshipped
　　　him,
Saying: Lord, help me! And he answered me,
It is not meet to take the children's bread
And cast it unto dogs! Truth, Lord, I said;
And yet the dogs may eat the crumbs which fall
From off their master's table; and he turned,
And answered me; and said to me: O woman,
Great is thy faith; then be it unto thee,
Even as thou wilt. And from that very hour
Thou wast made whole, my darling! my delight!

#### THE DAUGHTER.

There came upon my dark and troubled mind
A calm, as when the tumult of the city
Suddenly ceases, and I lie and hear
The silver trumpets of the Temple blowing
Their welcome to the Sabbath.   Still I wonder,
That one who was so far away from me,
And could not see me, by his thought alone
Had power to heal me.   O that I could see him!

#### THE MOTHER.

Perhaps thou wilt; for I have brought thee here
To keep the holy Passover, and lay
Thine offering of thanksgiving on the altar.
Thou mayst both see and hear him.   Hark!

#### VOICES *afar off.*

Hosanna!

#### THE DAUGHTER.

A crowd comes pouring through the city gate!
O mother, look!

#### VOICES *in the street.*

Hosanna to the Son
Of David!

#### THE DAUGHTER.

A great multitude of people
Fills all the street; and riding on an ass
Comes one of noble aspect, like a king!

The people spread their garments in the way,
And scatter branches of the palm-trees!

#### VOICES.

Blessed
Is he that cometh in the name of the Lord!
Hosanna in the highest!

#### OTHER VOICES.

Who is this?

#### VOICES.

Jesus of Nazareth!

#### THE DAUGHTER.

Mother, it is he!

#### VOICES.

He hath called Lazarus of Bethany
Out of his grave, and raised him from the dead!
Hosanna in the highest!

#### PHARISEES.

Ye perceive
That nothing we prevail.  Behold, the world
Is all gone after him!

#### THE DAUGHTER.

What majesty,
What power is in that care-worn countenance!
What sweetness, what compassion!  I no longer
Wonder that he hath healed me!

VOICES.

           Peace in heaven,
And glory in the highest!

PHARISEES.

           Rabbi! Rabbi!
Rebuke thy followers!

CHRISTUS.

           Should they hold their peace
The very stones beneath us would cry out!

THE DAUGHTER.

All hath passed by me like a dream of wonder!
But I have seen him, and have heard his voice,
And I am satisfied! I ask no more!

## II.

### SOLOMON'S PORCH.

#### GAMALIEL THE SCRIBE.

WHEN Rabban Simeon, upon whom be peace!
Taught in these Schools, he boasted that his pen
Had written no word that he could call his own,
But wholly and always had been consecrated
To the transcribing of the Law and Prophets.
He used to say, and never tired of saying,
The world itself was built upon the Law.

And ancient Hillel said, that whosoever
Gains a good name, gains something for himself,
But he who gains a knowledge of the Law
Gains everlasting life.   And they spake truly.
Great is the Written Law ; but greater still
The Unwritten, the Traditions of the Elders,
The lovely words of Levites, spoken first
To Moses on the Mount, and handed down
From mouth to mouth, in one unbroken sound
And sequence of divine authority,
The voice of God resounding through the ages.

The Written Law is water ; the Unwritten
Is precious wine ; the Written Law is salt,
The Unwritten costly spice ; the Written Law
Is but the body ; the Unwritten, the soul
That quickens it, and makes it breathe and live.

I can remember, many years ago,
A little bright-eyed school-boy, a mere stripling,
Son of a Galilean carpenter,
From Nazareth, I think, who came one day
And sat here in the Temple with the Scribes,
Hearing us speak, and asking many questions,
And we were all astonished at his quickness.
And when his mother came, and said : Behold
Thy father and I have sought thee, sorrowing ;
He looked as one astonished, and made answer !
How is it that ye sought me ?   Wist ye not

That I must be about my Father's business?
Often since then I see him here among us,
Or dream I see him, with his upraised face
Intent and eager, and I often wonder
Unto what manner of manhood he hath grown!
Perhaps a poor mechanic, like his father,
Lost in his little Galilean village
And toiling at his craft, to die unknown
And be no more remembered among men.

CHRISTUS *in the outer court.*

The Scribes and Pharisees sit in Moses' seat;
All, therefore, whatsoever they command you,
Observe and do; but follow not their works;
They say and do not. They bind heavy burdens
And very grievous to be borne, and lay them
Upon men's shoulders, but they move them not
With so much as a finger!

GAMALIEL, *looking forth.*
                    Who is this
Exhorting in the outer courts so loudly?

CHRISTUS.

Their works they do for to be seen of men.
They make broad their phylacteries, and enlarge
The borders of their garments, and they love
The uppermost rooms at feasts, and the chief seats
In Synagogues, and greetings in the markets,
And to be called of all men Rabbi, Rabbi!

GAMALIEL.

It is that loud and turbulent Galilean,
That came here at the Feast of Dedication,
And stirred the people up to break the Law!

CHRISTUS.

Woe unto you, ye Scribes and Pharisees,
Ye hypocrites! for ye shut up the kingdom
Of heaven, and neither go ye in yourselves
Nor suffer them that are entering to go in!

GAMALIEL.

How eagerly the people throng and listen,
As if his ribald words were words of wisdom!

CHRISTUS.

Woe unto you, ye Scribes and Pharisees,
Ye hypocrites! for ye devour the houses
Of widows, and for pretence ye make long prayers;
Therefore shall ye receive the more damnation.

GAMALIEL.

This brawler is no Jew, — he is a vile
Samaritan, and hath an unclean spirit!

CHRISTUS.

Woe unto you, ye Scribes and Pharisees,
Ye hypocrites! ye compass sea and land
To make one proselyte, and when he is made

Ye make him twofold more the child of hell
Than you yourselves are !

GAMALIEL.

O my father's father !
Hillel of blessed memory, hear and judge !

CHRISTUS.

Woe unto you, ye Scribes and Pharisees,
Ye hypocrites ! for ye pay tithe of mint,
Of anise and of cumin, and omit
The weightier matters of the law of God,
Judgment and faith and mercy ; and all these
Ye ought to have done, nor leave undone the others !

GAMALIEL.

O Rabban Simeon ! how must thy bones
Stir in their grave to hear such blasphemies !

CHRISTUS.

Woe unto you, ye Scribes and Pharisees,
Ye hypocrites ! for ye make clean and sweet
The outside of the cup and of the platter,
But they within are full of all excess !

GAMALIEL.

Patience of God ! canst thou endure so long ?
Or art thou deaf, or gone upon a journey ?

CHRISTUS.

Woe unto you, ye Scribes and Pharisees,
Ye hypocrites ! for ye are very like
To whited sepulchres, which indeed appear
Beautiful outwardly, but are within
Filled full of dead men's bones and all unclean-
ness!

GAMALIEL.

Am I awake ?   Is this Jerusalem ?
And are these Jews that throng and stare and
listen ?

CHRISTUS.

Woe unto you, ye Scribes and Pharisees,
Ye hypocrites ! because ye build the tombs
Of Prophets, and adorn the sepulchres
Of righteous men, and say : If we had lived
When lived our fathers, we would not have been
Partakers with them in the blood of Prophets.
So ye be witnesses unto yourselves,
That ye are children of them that killed the
Prophets !
Fill ye up then the measure of your fathers.
I send unto you Prophets and Wise Men,
And Scribes, and some ye crucify, and some
Scourge in your Synagogues, and persecute
From city to city ; that on you may come
The righteous blood that hath been shed on earth,
From the blood of righteous Abel to the blood

Of Zacharias, son of Barachias,
Ye slew between the Temple and the altar!

### GAMALIEL.

O, had I here my subtle dialectician,
My little Saul of Tarsus, the tent-maker,
Whose wit is sharper than his needle's point,
He would delight to foil this noisy wrangler!

### CHRISTUS.

Jerusalem! Jerusalem! O thou
That killest the Prophets, and that stonest them
Which are sent unto thee, how often would I
Have gathered together thy children, as a hen
Gathereth her chickens underneath her wing,
And ye would not!   Behold, your house is left
Unto you desolate!

### THE PEOPLE.

This is a Prophet!
This is the Christ that was to come!

### GAMALIEL.

Ye fools!
Think ye, shall Christ come out of Galilee?

8

## III.

### LORD, IS IT I?

#### CHRISTUS.

ONE of you shall betray me.

#### THE DISCIPLES.

Is it I?
Lord, is it I?

#### CHRISTUS.

One of the Twelve it is
That dippeth with me in this dish his hand;
He shall betray me.   Lo, the Son of Man
Goeth indeed as it is written of him;
But woe shall be unto that man by whom
He is betrayed!   Good were it for that man
If he had ne'er been born!

#### JUDAS ISCARIOT.

Lord, is it I?

#### CHRISTUS.

Ay, thou hast said.   And that thou doest, do
   quickly.

#### JUDAS ISCARIOT, *going out.*

Ah, woe is me!

CHRISTUS.

           All ye shall be offended
Because of me this night; for it is written :
Awake, O sword against my shepherd ! . Smite
The shepherd, saith the Lord of hosts, and scat-
    tered
Shall be the sheep ! — But after I am risen
I go before you into Galilee.

PETER.

O Master ! though all men shall be offended
Because of thee, yet will not I be !

CHRISTUS.

              Simon,
Behold how Satan hath desired to have you,
That he may sift you as one sifteth wheat !
Whither I go thou canst not follow me
Not now ; — but thou shalt follow me hereafter.

PETER.

Wherefore can I not follow thee ?   I am ready
To go with thee to prison and to death.

CHRISTUS.

Verily say I unto thee, this night,
Ere the cock crow, thou shalt deny me thrice !

PETER.

Though I should die, yet will I not deny thee.

CHRISTUS.

When first I sent you forth without a purse
Or scrip, or shoes, did ye lack anything?

THE DISCIPLES.

Not anything.

CHRISTUS.

But he that hath a purse,
Now let him take it, and likewise his scrip;
And he that hath no sword, let him go sell
His clothes and buy one. That which hath been
written
Must be accomplished now: He hath poured out
His soul even unto death; he hath been numbered
With the transgressors, and himself hath borne
The sin of many, and made intercession
For the transgressors. And here have an end
The things concerning me.

PETER.

Behold, O Lord,
Behold, here are two swords!

CHRISTUS.

It is enough.

## IV.

### THE GARDEN OF GETHSEMANE.

#### CHRISTUS.

My spirit is exceeding sorrowful
Even unto death ! Tarry ye here and watch.

*He goes apart.*

#### PETER.

Under this ancient olive-tree, that spreads
Its broad centennial branches like a tent,
Let us lie down and rest.

#### JOHN.

What are those torches,
That glimmer on Brook Kedron there below us ?

#### JAMES.

It is some marriage feast ; the joyful maidens
Go out to meet the bridegroom.

#### PETER.

I am weary.
The struggles of this day have overcome me.

*They sleep.*

#### CHRISTUS, *falling on his face.*

Father ! all things are possible to thee, —

O let this cup pass from me ! Nevertheless
Not as I will, but as thou wilt, be done !

*Returning to the Disciples.*

What ! could ye not watch with me for one hour ?
O watch and pray, that ye may enter not
Into temptation. For the spirit indeed
Is willing, but the flesh is weak !

JOHN.

Alas !
It is for sorrow that our eyes are heavy. —
I see again the glimmer of those torches
Among the olives ; they are coming hither.

JAMES.

Outside the garden wall the path divides ;
Surely they come not hither.

*They sleep again.*

CHRISTUS, *as before.*

O my Father !
If this cup may not pass away from me,
Except I drink of it, thy will be done.

*Returning to the Disciples.*

Sleep on ; and take your rest !

JOHN.

Beloved Master,
Alas ! we know not what to answer thee !

It is for sorrow that our eyes are heavy. —
Behold, the torches now encompass us.

### JAMES.

They do but go about the garden wall,
Seeking for some one, or for something lost.

*They sleep again.*

### CHRISTUS, *as before.*

If this cup may not pass away from me,
Except I drink of it, thy will be done.

*Returning to the Disciples.*

It is enough !   Behold, the Son of Man
Hath been betrayed into the hands of sinners !
The hour is come.   Rise up, let us be going ;
For he that shall betray me is at hand.

### JOHN.

Ah me !   See, from his forehead, in the torchlight,
Great drops of blood are falling to the ground !

### PETER.

What lights are these?   What torches glare and
glisten
Upon the swords and armor of these men ?
And there among them Judas Iscariot !

*He smites the servant of the High-Priest with his sword.*

### CHRISTUS.

Put up thy sword into its sheath ; for they

That take the sword shall perish with the sword.
The cup my Father hath given me to drink,
Shall I not drink it?   Think'st thou that I cannot
Pray to my Father, and that he shall give me
More than twelve legions of angels presently?

JUDAS *to* CHRISTUS, *kissing him.*

Hail, Master! hail!

CHRISTUS.

                    Friend, wherefore art thou come?
Whom seek ye?

CAPTAIN OF THE TEMPLE.

Jesus of Nazareth.

CHRISTUS.

                              I am he.
Are ye come hither as against a thief,
With swords and staves to take me?   When I daily
Was with you in the Temple, ye stretched forth
No hands to take me!   But this is your hour,
And this the power of darkness.   If ye seek
Me only, let these others go their way.

*The Disciples depart.* CHRISTUS *is bound and led away.
A certain young man follows him, having a linen cloth cast
about his body.   They lay hold of him, and the young man
flees from them naked.*

## V.

### THE PALACE OF CAIAPHAS.

PHARISEES.

WHAT do we?   Clearly something must we do,
For this man worketh many miracles.

CAIAPHAS.

I am informed that he is a mechanic ;
A carpenter's son ; a Galilean peasant,
Keeping disreputable company.

PHARISEES.

The people say that here in Bethany
He hath raised up a certain Lazarus,
Who had been dead three days.

CAIAPHAS.

                                        Impossible !
There is no resurrection of the dead ;
This Lazarus should be taken, and put to death
As an impostor.   If this Galilean
Would be content to stay in Galilee,
And preach in country towns, I should not heed
        him.
But when he comes up to Jerusalem
Riding in triumph, as I am informed,

And drives the money-changers from the Temple,
That is another matter.

PHARISEES.

If we thus
Let him alone, all will believe on him,
And then the Romans come and take away
Our place and nation.

CAIAPHAS.

Ye know nothing at all.
Simon Ben Camith, my great predecessor,
On whom be peace! would have dealt presently
With such a demagogue.   I shall no less.
The man must die.   Do ye consider not
It is expedient that one man should die,
Not the whole nation perish?   What is death?
It differeth from sleep but in duration.
We sleep and wake again; an hour or two
Later or earlier, and it matters not,
And if we never wake it matters not;
When we are in our graves we are at peace,
Nothing can wake us or disturb us more.
There is no resurrection.

PHARISEES, *aside.*

O most faithful
Disciple of Hircanus Maccabæus,
Will nothing but complete annihilation
Comfort and satisfy thee?

CAIAPHAS.

                    While ye are talking
And plotting, and contriving how to take him,
Fearing the people, and so doing naught,
I, who fear not the people, have been acting ;
Have taken this Prophet, this young Nazarene,
Who by Beelzebub the Prince of devils
Casteth out devils, and doth raise the dead,
That might as well be dead, and left in peace.
Annas my father-in-law hath sent him hither.
I hear the guard.   Behold your Galilean !

CHRISTUS *is brought in bound.*

SERVANT, *in the vestibule.*

Why art thou up so late, my pretty damsel ?

DAMSEL.

Why art thou up so early, pretty man ?
It is not cock-crow yet, and art thou stirring ?

SERVANT.

What brings thee here ?

DAMSEL.

                    What brings the rest of you ?

SERVANT.

Come here and warm thy hands.

DAMSEL *to* PETER.

       Art thou not also
One of this man's disciples?

PETER.

       I am not.

DAMSEL.

Now surely thou art also one of them;
Thou art a Galilean, and thy speech
Bewrayeth thee.

PETER.

    Woman, I know him not!

CAIAPHAS *to* CHRISTUS, *in the Hall.*

Who art thou? Tell us plainly of thyself
And of thy doctrines, and of thy disciples.

CHRISTUS.

Lo, I have spoken openly to the world,
I have taught ever in the Synagogue,
And in the Temple, where the Jews resort;
In secret have said nothing. Wherefore then
Askest thou me of this? Ask them that heard me
What I have said to them. Behold they know
What I have said!

OFFICER, *striking him.*

      What, fellow! answerest thou
The High-Priest so?

CHRISTUS.

If I have spoken evil,
Bear witness of the evil; but if well,
Why smitest thou me?

CAIAPHAS.

Where are the witnesses?
Let them say what they know.

THE TWO FALSE WITNESSES.

We heard him say:
I will destroy this Temple made with hands,
And will within three days build up another
Made without hands.

SCRIBES *and* PHARISEES.

He is o'erwhelmed with shame
And cannot answer!

CAIAPHAS.

Dost thou answer nothing?
What is this thing they witness here against thee?

SCRIBES *and* PHARISEES.

He holds his peace.

CAIAPHAS.

Tell us, art thou the Christ?
I do adjure thee by the living God,
Tell us, art thou indeed the Christ?

CHRISTUS.

I am.

Hereafter shall ye see the Son of Man
Sit on the right hand of the power of God,
And come in clouds of heaven !

CAIAPHAS, *rending his clothes.*

It is enough.

He hath spoken blasphemy !   What further need
Have we of witnesses ?   Now ye have heard
His blasphemy.   What think ye ?   Is he guilty ?

SCRIBES *and* PHARISEES.

Guilty of death !

KINSMAN OF MALCHUS *to* PETER, *in the vestibule.*

Surely I know thy face,
Did I not see thee in the garden with him ?

PETER.

How couldst thou see me ?   I swear unto thee
I do not know this man of whom ye speak !

*The cock crows.*

Hark ! the cock crows !   That sorrowful, pale face
Seeks for me in the crowd, and looks at me,
As if he would remind me of those words :
Ere the cock crow thou shalt deny me thrice !

*Goes out weeping.*   CHRISTUS *is blindfolded and buffeted.*

AN OFFICER, *striking him with his palm.*

Prophesy unto us, thou Christ, thou Prophet!
Who is it smote thee?

CAIAPHAS.

Lead him unto Pilate!

## VI.

### PONTIUS PILATE.

#### PILATE.

WHOLLY incomprehensible to me,
Vainglorious, obstinate, and given up
To unintelligible old traditions,
And proud, and self-conceited are these Jews!
Not long ago, I marched the legions down
From Cæsarea to their winter-quarters
Here in Jerusalem, with the effigies
Of Cæsar on their ensigns, and a tumult
Arose among these Jews, because their Law
Forbids the making of all images!
They threw themselves upon the ground with wild
Expostulations, bared their necks, and cried
That they would sooner die than have their Law
Infringed in any manner; as if Numa
Were not as great as Moses, and the Laws
Of the Twelve Tables as their Pentateuch!

And then, again, when I desired to span
Their valley with an aqueduct, and bring
A rushing river in to wash the city
And its inhabitants, — they all rebelled
As if they had been herds of unwashed swine !
Thousands and thousands of them got together
And raised so great a clamor round my doors,
That, fearing violent outbreak, I desisted,
And left them to their wallowing in the mire.

And now here comes the reverend Sanhedrim
Of lawyers, priests, and Scribes and Pharisees
Like old and toothless mastiffs, that can bark,
But cannot bite, howling their accusations
Against a mild enthusiast, who hath preached
I know not what new doctrine, being King
Of some vague kingdom in the other world,
That hath no more to do with Rome and Cæsar
Than I have with the patriarch Abraham !
Finding this man to be a Galilean
I sent him straight to Herod, and I hope
That is the last of it ; but if it be not,
I still have power to pardon and release him,
As is the custom at the Passover,
And so accommodate the matter smoothly,
Seeming to yield to them, yet saving him ;
A prudent and sagacious policy
For Roman Governors in the Provinces.

Incomprehensible, fanatic people !
Ye have a God, who seemeth like yourselves
Incomprehensible, dwelling apart,
Majestic, cloud-encompassed, clothed in darkness !
One whom ye fear, but love not ; yet ye have
No Goddesses to soften your stern lives,
And make you tender unto human weakness,
While we of Rome have everywhere around us
Our amiable divinities, that haunt
The woodlands, and the waters, and frequent
Our households, with their sweet and gracious
      presence !
I will go in, and while these Jews are wrangling,
Read my Ovidius on the Art of Love.

## VII.

### BARABBAS IN PRISON.

BARABBAS, *to his fellow-prisoners.*

BARABBAS is my name,
Barabbas, the Son of Shame,
    Is the meaning I suppose ;
I 'm no better than the best,
And whether worse than the rest
    Of my fellow-men, who knows ?

I was once, to say it in brief,
A highwayman, a robber chief,
    In the open light of day.

So much I am free to confess;
But all men, more or less,
    Are robbers in their way.

From my cavern in the crags,
From my lair of leaves and flags,
    I could see, like ants, below,
The camels with their load
Of merchandise, on the road
    That leadeth to Jericho.

And I struck them unaware,
As an eagle from the air
    Drops down upon bird or beast;
And I had my heart's desire
Of the merchants of Sidon and Tyre,
    And Damascus and the East.

But it is not for that I fear;
It is not for that I am here
    In these iron fetters bound;
Sedition! that is the word
That Pontius Pilate heard,
    And he liketh not the sound.

What, think ye, would he care
For a Jew slain here or there,
    Or a plundered caravan?
But Cæsar!— ah, that is a crime,

To the uttermost end of time
   Shall not be forgiven to man.

Therefore was Herod wroth
With Matthias Margaloth,
   And burned him for a show !
Therefore his wrath did smite
Judas the Gaulonite,
   And his followers, as ye know.

For that cause, and no more,
Am I here, as I said before ;
   For one unlucky night,
Jucundus, the captain of horse,
Was upon us with all his force,
   And I was caught in the fight.

I might have fled with the rest,
But my dagger was in the breast
   Of a Roman equerry ;
As we rolled there in the street,
They bound me, hands and feet ;
   And this is the end of me.

Who cares for death ?   Not I !
A thousand times I would die,
   Rather than suffer wrong !
Already those women of mine
Are mixing the myrrh and the wine ;
   I shall not be with you long.

## VIII.

### ECCE HOMO.

PILATE, *on the Tessellated Pavement in front of his Palace.*

YE have brought unto me this man, as one
Who doth pervert the people ; and behold !
I have examined him, and found no fault
Touching the things whereof ye do accuse him.
No, nor yet Herod ; for I sent you to him,
And nothing worthy of death he findeth in him.
Ye have a custom at the Passover,
That one condemned to death shall be released.
Whom will ye, then, that I release to you ?
Jesus Barabbas, called the Son of Shame,
Or Jesus, Son of Joseph, called the Christ ?

### THE PEOPLE, *shouting.*

Not this man, but Barabbas !

### PILATE.
                              What then will ye
That I should do with him that is called Christ ?

### THE PEOPLE.
Crucify him !

### PILATE.
                    Why, what evil hath he done ?
Lo, I have found no cause of death in him ;
I will chastise him, and then let him go.

THE PEOPLE, *more vehemently.*

Crucify him! crucify him!

A MESSENGER, *to* PILATE.

                Thy wife sends
This message to thee : — Have thou naught to do
With that just man ; for I this day in dreams
Have suffered many things because of him.

PILATE, *aside.*

The Gods speak to us in our dreams! I tremble
At what I have to do! O Claudia,
How shall I save him? Yet one effort more,
Or he must perish!

        *Washes his hands before them.*

            I am innocent
Of the blood of this just person ; see ye to it!

THE PEOPLE.

Let his blood be on us and on our children!

VOICES, *within the Palace.*

Put on thy royal robes ; put on thy crown,
And take thy sceptre! Hail, thou King of the
    Jews!

PILATE.

I bring him forth to you, that ye may know
I find no fault in him. Behold the man!

CHRISTUS *is led in, with the purple robe and crown of thorns.*

CHIEF PRIESTS *and* OFFICERS.

Crucify him ! crucify him !

PILATE.

      Take ye him ;
I find no fault in him.

CHIEF PRIESTS.

    We have a Law,
And by our Law he ought to die ; because
He made himself to be the Son of God.

PILATE, *aside.*

Ah ! there are Sons of God, and demi-gods
More than ye know, ye ignorant High-Priests !

*To* CHRISTUS.

Whence art thou ?

CHIEF PRIESTS.

      Crucify him ! crucify him !

PILATE, *to* CHRISTUS.

Dost thou not answer me ? Dost thou not know
That I have power enough to crucify thee ?
That I have also power to set thee free ?

CHRISTUS.

Thou couldest have no power at all against me
Except that it were given thee from above ;

Therefore hath he that sent me unto thee
The greater sin.

CHIEF PRIESTS.

If thou let this man go,
Thou art not Cæsar's friend.   For whosoever
Maketh himself a King, speaks against Cæsar.

PILATE.

Ye Jews, behold your King !

CHIEF PRIESTS.

Away with him !
Crucify him !

PILATE.

Shall I crucify your King ?

CHIEF PRIESTS.

We have no King but Cæsar !

PILATE.

Take him, then,
Take him, ye cruel and bloodthirsty Priests,
More merciless than the plebeian mob,
Who pity and spare the fainting gladiator
Blood-stained in Roman amphitheatres, —
Take him, and crucify him if ye will ;
But if the immortal Gods do ever mingle
With the affairs of mortals, which I doubt not,
And hold the attribute of justice dear,

They will commission the Eumenides
To scatter you to the four winds of heaven,
Exacting tear for tear, and blood for blood.
Here, take ye this inscription, Priests, and nail it
Upon the cross, above your victim's head :
Jesus of Nazareth, King of the Jews.

#### CHIEF PRIESTS.

Nay, we entreat! write not, the King of the Jews;
But that he said : I am the King of the Jews!

#### PILATE.

Enough.   What I have written, I have written!


## IX.

### ACELDAMA.

#### JUDAS ISCARIOT.

Lost! lost! forever lost !   I have betrayed
The innocent blood !   O God ! if thou art love,
Why didst thou leave me naked to the tempter ?
Why didst thou not commission thy swift lightning
To strike me dead ? or why did I not perish
With those by Herod slain, the innocent children
Who went with playthings in their little hands
Into the darkness of the other world,
As if to bed ?   Or wherefore was I born,

If thou in thy foreknowledge didst perceive
All that I am, and all that I must be ?
I know I am not generous, am not gentle
Like other men ; but I have tried to be,
And I have failed.   I thought by following Him,
I should grow like him ; but the unclean spirit
That from my childhood up hath tortured me
Hath been too cunning and too strong for me.
Am I to blame for this?   Am I to blame
Because I cannot love, and ne'er have known
The love of woman or the love of children ?
It is a curse and a fatality,
A mark, that hath been set upon my forehead,
That none shall slay me, for it were a mercy
That I were dead, or never had been born.

Too late ! too late ! I shall not see him more
Among the living.   That sweet, patient face
Will never more rebuke me, nor those lips
Repeat the words : One of you shall betray me !
It stung me into madness.   How I loved,
Yet hated him !   But in the other world !
I will be there before him, and will wait
Until he comes, and fall down on my knees
And kiss his feet, imploring pardon, pardon !

I heard him say : All sins shall be forgiven,
Except the sin against the Holy Ghost.
That shall not be forgiven in this world,

Nor in the world to come.   Is that my sin?
Have I offended so there is no hope
Here nor hereafter?   That I soon shall know.
O God, have mercy!   Christ have mercy on me!

*Throws himself headlong from the cliff.*

## X.

### THE THREE CROSSES.

#### MANAHEM, THE ESSENIAN.

THREE crosses in this noonday night uplifted,
Three human figures, that in mortal pain
Gleam white against the supernatural darkness;
Two thieves, that writhe in torture, and between
    them
The Suffering Messiah, the Son of Joseph,
Ay, the Messiah Triumphant, Son of David!
A crown of thorns on that dishonored head!
Those hands that healed the sick now pierced with
    nails,
Those feet that wandered homeless through the
    world
Now crossed and bleeding, and at rest forever!
And the three faithful Maries, overwhelmed
By this great sorrow, kneeling, praying, weeping!
O Joseph Caiaphas, thou great High-Priest,
How wilt thou answer for this deed of blood?

SCRIBES *and* ELDERS.

Thou that destroyest the Temple, and dost build it
In three days, save thyself; and if thou be
The Son of God, come down now from the cross.

CHIEF PRIESTS.

Others he saved, himself he cannot save!
Let Christ the King of Israel descend
That we may see and believe!

SCRIBES *and* ELDERS.

      In God he trusted;
Let him deliver him, if he will have him,
And we will then believe.

CHRISTUS.

     Father! forgive them;
They know not what they do.

THE IMPENITENT THIEF.

      If thou be Christ,
O save thyself and us!

THE PENITENT THIEF.

     Remember me,
Lord, when thou comest into thine own kingdom.

CHRISTUS.

This day shalt thou be with me in Paradise.

### MANAHEM.

Golgotha! Golgotha!   O the pain and darkness!
O the uplifted cross, that shall forever
Shine through the darkness, and shall conquer pain
By the triumphant memory of this hour!

### SIMON MAGUS.

O Nazarene! I find thee here at last!
Thou art no more a phantom unto me!
This is the end of one who called himself
The Son of God!   Such is the fate of those
Who preach new doctrines.   'T is not what he did,
But what he said, hath brought him unto this.
I will speak evil of no dignitaries.
This is my hour of triumph, Nazarene!

### THE YOUNG RULER.

This is the end of him who said to me:
Sell that thou hast, and give unto the poor!
This is the treasure in heaven he promised me!

### CHRISTUS.

*Eloi, Eloi, lama sabacthani!*

### A SOLDIER, *preparing the hyssop.*

He calleth for Elias!

### ANOTHER.

Nay, let be!
See if Elias now will come to save him!

CHRISTUS.

I thirst.

A SOLDIER.

Give him the wormwood !

CHRISTUS, *with a loud cry, bowing his head.*

It is finished !

## XI.

### THE TWO MARIES.

MARY MAGDALENE.

WE have arisen early, yet the sun
O'ertakes us ere we reach the sepulchre,
To wrap the body of our blessed Lord
With our sweet spices.

MARY, MOTHER OF JAMES.

Lo, this is the garden,
And yonder is the sepulchre.   But who
Shall roll away the stone for us to enter?

MARY MAGDALENE.

It hath been rolled away !   The sepulchre
Is open !   Ah, who hath been here before us,
When we rose early, wishing to be first?

MARY, MOTHER OF JAMES.

I am affrighted!

MARY MAGDALENE.

Hush! I will stoop down
And look within.   There is a young man sitting
On the right side, clothed in a long white garment!
It is an angel!

THE ANGEL.

Fear not; ye are seeking
Jesus of Nazareth, which was crucified.
Why do ye seek the living among the dead?
He is no longer here; he is arisen!
Come see the place where the Lord lay!   Remember
How he spake unto you in Galilee,
Saying: The Son of Man must be delivered
Into the hands of sinful men; by them
Be crucified, and the third day rise again!
But go your way, and say to his disciples,
He goeth before you into Galilee;
There shall ye see him as he said to you.

MARY, MOTHER OF JAMES.

I will go swiftly for them.

MARY MAGDALENE, *alone, weeping.*

They have taken
My Lord away from me, and now I know not

Where they have laid him ! Who is there to tell
    me ?
This is the gardener. Surely he must know.

#### CHRISTUS.

Woman, why weepest thou ? Whom seekest thou ?

#### MARY MAGDALENE.

They have taken my Lord away ; I cannot find him.
O Sir, if thou have borne him hence, I pray thee
Tell me where thou hast laid him.

#### CHRISTUS.

                      Mary !

#### MARY MAGDALENE.

                        Rabboni !


## XII.

### THE SEA OF GALILEE.

#### NATHANAEL, *in the ship.*

ALL is now ended.

#### JOHN.

            Nay, he is arisen.
I ran unto the tomb, and stooping down
Looked in, and saw the linen grave-clothes lying,
Yet dared not enter.

PETER.

I went in, and saw
The napkin that had been about his head,
Not lying with the other linen clothes,
But wrapped together in a separate place.

THOMAS.

And I have seen him.   I have seen the print
Of nails upon his hands, and thrust my hands
Into his side.   I know he is arisen ;
But where are now the kingdom and the glory
He promised unto us ?   We have all dreamed
That we were princes, and we wake to find
We are but fishermen.

PETER.

Who should have been
Fishers of men !

JOHN.

We have come back again
To the old life, the peaceful life, among
The white towns of the Galilean lake.

PETER.

They seem to me like silent sepulchres
In the gray light of morning !   The old life,
Yea, the old life ! for we have toiled all night
And have caught nothing.

JOHN.

Do ye see a man
Standing upon the beach and beckoning?
'T is like an apparition.   He hath kindled
A fire of coals, and seems to wait for us.
He calleth.

CHRISTUS, *from the shore.*

Children, have ye any meat?

PETER

Alas!   We have caught nothing.

CHRISTUS.

Cast the net
On the right side of the ship, and ye shall find.

PETER.

How that reminds me of the days gone by,
And one who said: Launch out into the deep,
And cast your nets!

NATHANAEL.

We have but let them down
And they are filled, so that we cannot draw them!

JOHN.

It is the Lord!

10

PETER, *girding his fisher's coat about him.*

     He said : When I am risen
I will go before you into Galilee !

*He casts himself into the lake.*

### JOHN.

There is no fear in love ; for perfect love
Casteth out fear.   Now then, if ye are men,
Put forth your strength ; we are not far from shore ;
The net is heavy, but breaks not.   All is safe.

### PETER, *on the shore.*

Dear Lord ! I heard thy voice and could not wait.
Let me behold thy face, and kiss thy feet !
Thou art not dead, thou livest !   Again I see thee.
Pardon, dear Lord !   I am a sinful man ;
I have denied thee thrice.   Have mercy on me !

### THE OTHERS, *coming to land.*

Dear Lord ! stay with us ! cheer us ! comfort us !
Lo ! we again have found thee !   Leave us not !

### CHRISTUS.

Bring hither of the fish that ye have caught,
And come and eat !

### JOHN.

     Behold ! he breaketh bread
As he was wont.   From his own blessed hands
Again we take it.

CHRISTUS.

Simon, son of Jonas,
Lovest thou me, more than these others?

PETER.

Yea,
More, Lord, than all men ; even more than these.
Thou knowest that I love thee.

CHRISTUS.

Feed my lambs.

THOMAS, *aside.*

How more than we do ?   He remaineth ever
Self-confident and boastful as before.
Nothing will cure him.

CHRISTUS.

Simon, son of Jonas,
Lovest thou me ?

PETER.

Yea, dearest Lord, I love thee.
Thou knowest that I love thee.

CHRISTUS.

Feed my sheep.

THOMAS, *aside.*

Again, the selfsame question, and the answer
Repeated with more vehemence.   Can the Master
Doubt if we love him ?

CHRISTUS.

Simon, son of Jonas,
Lovest thou me ?

PETER, *grieved.*

Dear Lord! thou knowest all things.
Thou knowest that I love thee.

CHRISTUS.

Feed my sheep.
When thou wast young thou girdedst thyself, and
    walkedst
Whither thou wouldst; but when thou shalt be old,
Thou shalt stretch forth thy hands, and other men
Shall gird and carry thee whither thou wouldst not.
Follow thou me!

JOHN, *aside.*

It is a prophecy
Of what death he shall die.

PETER, *pointing to* JOHN.

Tell me, O Lord,
And what shall this man do?

CHRISTUS.

And if I will
He tarry till I come, what is it to thee?
Follow thou me!

PETER.

Yea, I will follow thee, dear Lord and Master!
Will follow thee through fasting and temptation,
Through all thine agony and bloody sweat,
Thy cross and passion, even unto death!

# EPILOGUE

———◆———

## SYMBOLUM APOSTOLORUM.

### PETER.

I BELIEVE in God the Father Almighty;

### JOHN.

Maker of Heaven and Earth;

### JAMES.

And in Jesus Christ his only Son, our Lord;

### ANDREW.

Who was conceived by the Holy Ghost, born of
the Virgin Mary;

### PHILIP.

Suffered under Pontius Pilate, was crucified, dead
and buried;

### THOMAS.

And the third day he rose again from the dead;

### BARTHOLOMEW.

He ascended into Heaven, and sitteth on the right
hand of God, the Father Almighty;

### MATTHEW.

From thence he shall come to judge the quick and
the dead.

### JAMES, THE SON OF ALPHEUS.

I believe in the Holy Ghost; the holy Catholic
Church;

### SIMON ZELOTES.

The communion of Saints; the forgiveness of sins;

### JUDE.

The resurrection of the body;

### MATTHIAS.

And the Life Everlasting.

### THE END.

Cambridge: Printed by Welch, Bigelow, & Co.

### BARTHOLOMEW.

He ascended into Heaven, and sitteth on the right hand of God, the Father Almighty.

### MATTHEW.

From thence he shall come to judge the quick and the dead.

### JAMES, THE SON OF ALPHEUS.

I believe in the Holy Ghost; the Holy Catholic Church.

### SIMON ZELOTES.

The communion of Saints; the forgiveness of sins;

### JUDE.

The resurrection of the body;

### MATTHIAS.

And the Life Everlasting.

THE END.

Cambridge: Printed by W. H. Bigelow, & Co.